MASONIC LODGE

Zondervan
Guide to Cults &
Religious Movements

First Series

Unmasking the Cults   *by Alan W. Gomes*
Jehovah's Witnesses   *by Robert M. Bowman, Jr.*
Masonic Lodge   *by George A. Mather and Larry A. Nichols*
Mormonism   *by Kurt Van Gorden*
New Age Movement   *by Ron Rhodes*
Satanism   *by Bob and Gretchen Passantino*
Unification Church   *by J. Isamu Yamamoto*
Mind Sciences   *by Todd Ehrenborg*

Second Series

"Jesus Only" Churches   *by E. Calvin Beisner*
Astrology and Psychic Phenomena   *by André Kole and Terry Holley*
Goddess Worship, Witchcraft and Other Neo-Pagan Movements
   by Craig Hawkins
TM, Hare Krishna and Other Hindu-based Movements
   by Kurt Van Gorden
Dianetics and Scientology   *by Kurt Van Gorden*
Unitarian Universalism   *by Alan W. Gomes*
UFO Cults and Urantia   *by Kenneth Samples and Kevin Lewis*
Buddhism, Taoism and Other Far Eastern Movements
   by J. Isamu Yamamoto

ZONDERVAN
GUIDE to CULTS &
RELIGIOUS
MOVEMENTS

MASONIC LODGE

GEORGE A. MATHER
AND LARRY A. NICHOLS
Authors

Alan W. Gomes
Series Editor

ZondervanPublishingHouse
Grand Rapids, Michigan

A Division of HarperCollinsPublishers

Dedicated to the loving memory of Harold T. Dodge,
who was a past Massachusetts District Deputy Grand Master
and a 32nd Degree Consistory Order of the Eastern Star.
More important, he was a loving father and faithful
husband who now rests in Christ.

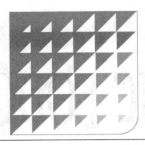

Masonic Lodge
Copyright © 1995 by George A. Mather and Larry A. Nichols

Requests for information should be addressed to:
 Zondervan Publishing House
 Grand Rapids, Michigan 49530.

Library of Congress Cataloging-in-Publication Data

Mather, George A.
  Masonic lodge / George A. Mather and Larry A. Nichols, authors.
      p. cm. — (Zondervan guide to cults & religious movements)
  Includes bibliographical references.
  ISBN: 0-310-70421-9 (pbk.)
      1. Freemasonry—Controversial literature. I. Nichols, Larry A.
  II. Title. II. Series: Zondervan guide to cults and religious movements.
  HS475.M38   1995
  366'.1—dc20   94-29238
                                                                         CIP

Edited by Patti Picardi
Interior design by Art Jacobs

Printed in the United States of America

95 96 97 98 99 00 /❖ DP/ 10 9 8 7 6 5 4 3 2 1

Contents

How to Use This Book

The *Zondervan Guide to Cults and Religious Movements* comprises sixteen volumes, treating many of the most important groups and belief systems confronting the Christian church today. This series distills the most important facts about each and presents a well-reasoned, cogent Christian response. The authors in this series are highly qualified, well-respected professional Christian apologists with considerable expertise on their topics.

For ease of use we have sought to maintain the same "look and feel" for all the books. We designed the structure and layout to help you find the information you need as quickly as possible.

All the volumes are written in outline form. This allows us to pack substantial content into a short book. The major divisions are basically the same from book to book. Each book contains an introduction to the cult, movement, or belief system. The introduction gives a brief history of the group, its organizational structure, and vital statistics such as membership. The theology section is arranged by doctrinal topic, such as God, Christ, sin, and salvation. The movement's position on each topic is set forth objectively, primarily from its own official writings. The group's teachings are then refuted point by point, followed by an affirmative presentation of what the Bible says about the doctrine. Following the theology section is a discussion of witnessing tips. While each witnessing encounter must be handled individually and sensitively, this section provides some helpful general guidelines, including both dos and don'ts. The books also have annotated bibliographies, listing works by the groups themselves as well as books written by Christians in response. Each book concludes with a parallel comparison chart. Arranged topically, the chart juxtaposes direct quotations from the cultic literature in the left column with the biblical refutation on the right.

One potential problem with a detailed outline is that it is easy to lose one's place in the overall structure. To overcome this problem we have provided graphical "signposts" at the top of the odd-numbered pages. Functioning like a "you are here" map in a shopping mall, these graphics show your place in the outline, including the sections that come before and after your current position. In the theology section we have also used "icons" in the margins to make clear at a glance whether the material is being presented from the cultic or Christian viewpoint. For example, in the Mormonism volume those portions of the outline presenting the Mormon position are indicated with a picture of the angel Moroni in the margin. The biblical view is shown by a drawing of a Bible.

We hope you will find these books useful as you seek "to give an answer to everyone who asks you to give the reason for the hope that you have" (1 Peter 3:15).

—Alan W. Gomes, Ph.D.
Series Editor

Part I:
Introduction

I. Historical Background

A. The Problem of Determining the Origin of Freemasonry

1. The history of the Masonic Lodge (also known as Freemasonry) is not easy to recount.

   According to Dr. Alvin Schmidt, one of the world's leading scholars on fraternal organizations, Freemasonry officially began in London, England in 1717 at the Goose and Gridiron Tavern.[1] This conclusion is supported by the consensus of scholars and historians.

2. Despite this scholarly consensus, the origin has been disputed by members of the craft[2] itself, who claim various origins dating back to the creation of humankind.

B. Spurious Masonic Accounts of Their History

1. The Masons claim ancient roots as a way of lending credibility and stature to their organization.

   a. Some well-known accounts

   (1) Freemasonry dates back to the time of Adam and Eve, and the fig leaves (Gen. 3:7) were actually the first Masonic "aprons" (aprons are used in initiatory ceremonies in Freemasonry).[3]

   (2) Freemasonry dates back to the time of Solomon who employed stone masons to construct the temple in Jerusalem.

   b. Other unsubstantiated claims

   (1) Freemasonry is tied to the builders of the Tower of Babel, or the story of Noah, or the account of the life of the biblical Seth.

   (2) Masons are the descendants of the Knights Templar.[4]

---

[1] Alvin Schmidt, *The Greenwood Encyclopedia of American Institutions: Fraternal Organizations* (Westport, Conn.: Greenwood Press, 1980), 120.

[2] "Craft" is a commonly used term for Freemasonary.

[3] Of course, the real reason for Adam and Eve sewing fig leaves was not to initiate themselves into the first fraternal organization, as many Masons believe. Rather, they were hastily trying to cover up their nakedness, as even a casual reading of the biblical text makes plain. Breaking God's command to not eat from the tree of the "knowledge of good and evil" had caused shame and the painful awareness that they had sinned against their creator.

[4] The Knights Templar were also called the Poor Fellow Soldiers of Christ. They were established in 1119 by a band of nine French knights who vowed to devote themselves to the protection of pilgrims traveling to Palestine. Many joined the ranks of the Templar and they became a powerful army. Feeling threatened, King Philip IV tried to destroy the Knights in the early fourteenth century. Pope Clement V also opposed the order and, in 1314, their grand master, Jacques de Molay, was burned at the stake.

(3) The Masonic edition of the Bible claims yet another link to antiquity when it states: "It is admitted that Freemasonry is descendent from the ancient mysteries. These were first arranged when the constellation Leo was at the Summer Solstice. Thus the antiquity of Freemasonry was written in the starry heavens."[5]

2. It is not surprising that Freemasonry incorporates its own story into various stories from the ancient sourcebook of Jews and Christians, namely the Bible. Historically, Freemasonry was born and bred upon the Christian soil of Western Europe after Christianity had been entrenched there for nearly eighteen centuries.

C. True Origins of Freemasonry

1. Historians trace the beginnings of the Lodge[6] back to London, England in the year 1717; the earliest recorded minutes of a meeting date back to 1723.[7]

2. Freemasonry encountered much opposition from the Roman Catholic Church due to its secretive nature, religious character, and rites.[8] (Freemasonry was never recognized as a Christian institution even though it enjoins such common Christian elements as morality, citizenship, and good ethical conduct.)

3. It was during this early period that James Anderson wrote his *Constitutions*, which revised a fourteenth-century stonemason's Christian guidebook entitled *Gothic Constitutions*.

   a. Anderson's work introduced elements of deism (see also Part II, section III.C.3–4).

   b. It also opened up the possibility for the formation of new Lodges as offshoots of the British system.

4. In 1717, James Anderson, George Payne, and Theopholis Desaguliers united their efforts to form the Grand Lodge; Lodges later sprang up in England and, on the continent, in Holland, Germany, France, and other European countries.

5. Attempts had been made to bring all the Lodges under one Supreme Lodge.

   a. This never took place.

   b. Each Lodge is governed by its own constitution and laws.

6. There are many instances where Grand Lodges have united to work together.

---

5 *The Holy Bible*, rev. ed. (John A. Hertel Co., 1957), p. 21.

6 In A.D. 1278 the word *lodge* originally referred to a storehouse where the stone masons kept their tools. It was a temporary structure located near the construction site (see Schmidt, *Fraternal Organizations*, 122).

7 Prior to this, guilds of stonemasons were formed during the Middle Ages. It was these craft guilds which were charged with the building of cathedrals and other lavish edifices.

8 For more on the response of various Christian denominations to Freemasonry, see Part II, Section I.D.2.

    a. For example, in 1912, the individual Lodges in Alexandria, Virginia united to form the George Washington Masonic National Memorial.

    b. Out of this effort, a conference sprang up which called together all the masters of the Grand Lodges throughout North America.

D. *The Lodge in North America*

  1. The United States

    a. Freemasonry experienced its greatest success in the United States. Indeed, few religions and social institutions of the world have overlooked America.

    b. The London Lodge chartered the first official Lodge in America: St. John's in Boston on July 30, 1733.

    c. The first indigenous Lodge was founded in Savannah, Georgia, in 1734.

    d. A Jew named Moses Michael Hays introduced the first Scottish Rite Freemasonry into the United States in the 1760s.[9]

    e. During the 1800s, several thousand Lodges were erected throughout the United States, making it a significant and powerful institution in America.

      (1) The Lodge has played a key role in American religious, political, and social life since then.

      (2) Men from all walks of life have been Lodge members. Among the prominent Masons in American culture are astronauts Edwin Aldrin, Virgil Grisson, and Leroy Cooper; actors John Wayne and Clark Gable; comedian Red Skelton; Henry Ford; John Philip Sousa; and General Douglas MacArthur. Fourteen United States presidents, including the nation's first, George Washington, eighteen vice presidents, and five chief justices of the Supreme Court were all Masons.

    f. Also during the 1800s, the Lodge underwent intense persecution. Mr. William Morgan appeared to be responsible for igniting the flames by passing out anti-masonic tracts and literature which exposed the Lodge's secrets and rituals.

    g. Morgan disappeared in 1826 and was never heard from again. His apparent death (many believed the Masons were responsible) only exacerbated the mounting anti-Lodge sentiment.

    h. Historian Sydney Ahlstrom observed that the Masons in America came largely from those European immigrants who were only nominally religious, unaffiliated, or anticlerical.[10]

      (1) Many of these immigrants brought with them memories of the church's hostile attitude toward the Lodge in Europe.

---

[9] For more on the Scottish Rite, see II.C. below.

[10] Sydney E. Alstrom, *A Religious History of the American People*, 2 vols. (Garden City, N.Y.: Image Books, 1975), 2:212.

      (2) Consequently, those who had a need for ritualism and community outside of the auspices of the Christian church satisfied that need through Lodge membership.

2. Canada and Other Migrations
   a. As the Lodge made its way through Europe, it also came to colonial America, Canada, and even into South America.
      (1) Canada's first Lodge was built at Capre Breton in 1745.
      (2) The Canadian Lodge played a major role in the establishment of the Jerusalem Lodge.[11]
   b. Lodges sprang up rapidly in other parts of the world as well, including Brazil, Israel, Mexico, the West Indies, and numerous other locations.
   c. Jews were allowed membership in the Lodge. The wording of *Constitutions* certainly seems to permit it.

II. The Masonic Families

A. The Blue Lodge

1. The Blue Lodge is regarded as the most original and authentic version of Freemasonry.
2. All Master Masons undergo initiation into the Blue Lodge[12] (i.e., a person first enters Freemasonry through the Blue Lodge).
3. There are some general requirements for Lodge membership.
   a. In general, membership in the Lodge, as well as the Scottish Rite, includes the requirement that the candidate be a white male of twenty-one years of age[13] (see the section on racism at II. F. below).
   b. Today some Lodges do allow black members, though many continue to resist black membership.
4. The Blue Lodge was formally called "The Order of Ancient, Free and Accepted Masons"; it is also variously known as "Symbolic Craft Masonry" and "Craft Masonry."
5. Members participate in oaths sworn in secrecy, never to be betrayed even under pain of death.
   a. Most Masons do not take the oaths literally or seriously.
   b. Many Masons, especially today, rehearse them as a matter of formality, and uncritically accept them as part of what it means to be a member of the Lodge.

---

[11] Many Masons believe that Jerusalem is where Freemasonry was born. It is therefore not suprising that Lodges would be erected in Jerusalem and the Holy Land in general.

[12] Initiation rites are described below.

[13] In France, the legal age is eighteen for Lodge membership.

6. The Blue Lodge has three degrees.

   a. Entered Apprentice

   b. Fellow Craft

   c. Master Mason

7. Acceptance into the Lodge presupposes a recommendation from a member.

   a. After a candidate is recommended, a report follows at a meeting and a vote is cast.

   b. If the member receives a "blackball" (negative vote), a "foul" is announced and a second vote is taken; if the candidate is blackballed a second time, he is rejected.

   c. If accepted, the candidate then begins to earn the degree of Entered Apprentice.

8. After participating in the required rituals for each of the degrees, and before receiving the Master Mason degree, the candidate swears an oath.

   a. The oath is ". . . I promise and swear, that I will not write, print, stamp, stain, hew, cut, carve, indent, paint, or engrave it [Masonic secrets] on anything movable or immovable . . . binding myself under no less penalty than to have my throat cut across, my tongue torn out by the roots, and my body buried in the rough sands of the sea at lower water mark . . . where the tide ebbs and flows twice in twenty-four hours; so help me God, and keep me steadfast in the due performance of the same."[14]

   b. Has this oath ever been carried out?

     (1) The Captain Morgan case (1826) in Batavia, New York, is one case offered by anti-Masons.

     (2) They claimed that Morgan's throat was slashed and he was dumped in Lake Ontario.

     (3) There is no substantial proof that Masons did this.

     (4) It must be remembered that the Morgan case occurred during the anti-Masonic period (1826–1840).

     (5) In the last few years, some Grand Lodges have actually done away with blood-curdling oaths.

9. Two other main branches of Freemasonry follow after one has achieved membership in the Blue Lodge.

   a. York Rite (see B. below)

   b. Scottish Rite (see C. below)

---

[14] This oath was recorded by Schmidt, *Fraternal Organizations*, 123.

B. The York Rite

1. After completing the degrees in the Blue Lodge, Masons may then choose to earn the higher degrees in one of two rites: the York and Scottish Rites.
2. Also called the "American Rite," the designation "York Rite" remains the most popular appellation.
3. The York Rite is probably the oldest form of Freemasonry.
   a. The rite takes its name from York, England.
   b. York was the seat of the Ancient York Grand Lodge.[15]
4. York Rite Masonry comprises three distinct bodies called Grand Chapters.
   a. Royal Arch Chapter[16]
   b. The Council of Royal and Select Masters
   c. The Commandery of Knights Templar
5. Comparison of York and Scottish Rite Masonry
   a. The three bodies of York Rite Masonry, noted above, constitute an important difference with the Scottish Rite which, according to Schmidt, is a "continuous entity, organizationally."[17]
   b. The York Rite contains ten additional degrees.
6. A Lodge of York Rite Masons is called a Chapter and each of its members are called Royal Arch Masons once they are initiated as such in the seventh degree (see 7.d.).
7. Four additional degrees after Master Mason are known as Chapter Degrees because they are awarded by the General Grand Chapter (GGC) of the York Rite.
   a. Mark Master (fourth degree)
      (1) The ritual involves the myth about finding the missing keystone in a pile of rubble in ancient Tyre.
      (2) The stone was engraved with symbols and proved to be the missing stone needed to complete the Temple (not accomplished, however, until the sixth degree).
   b. Past Master (fifth degree)
      This degree involves additional training in leadership skills.
   c. Most Excellent Master (sixth degree)
      The ritual involves the completion of Solomon's Temple.

---

[15] According to Alvin Schmidt, "The name of the York Rite, of Anglo-American origin, is considered by some to be a misnomer in that it reminds Masons of the ancient York Masons, an organization that came into being in 1756 in England as a result of the schism in Masonry. It ceased to exist in 1813." See "Freemasonry: A Way of Life," *Grand Lodge of New Mexico* 1, no.1 (Summer 1984): n.p.

[16] Important rites and degrees of Royal Arch Masonry are discussed in more detail at B.10. The features cited here are those which distinguish York Rite Freemasonry from all other forms.

[17] Schmidt, *Fraternal Organizations*, 137.

    d. Royal Arch Mason (seventh degree)

       The rites of this degree recall how three Most Excellent Masters are carried into captivity by Nebuchadnezzar, later returning from exile to rebuild the Temple.

8. The next three degrees awarded by the GGC (completely optional) each contain additional mythology surrounding the construction of Solomon's Temple.

    a. Royal Master (eighth degree)

    b. Select Master (ninth degree)

       In this degree, the candidate may choose to enter what is known as the Commandery, which comprises three Orders.

       (1) Order of the Red Cross

       (2) Order of the Knights of Malta

       (3) Order of the Knights Templar (the highest award in York Rite Masonry).

    c. Super Excellent Master (unnumbered degree)

9. The Degrees in York Rite Masonry are thus divided into three basic families or groups.

    a. Chapter Degrees, also known as Capitular, (degrees 4–7).

    b. Council Degrees, (degrees 8 and 9).

    c. Commandery Degrees (Red Cross, Knights of Malta, and Knights Templar).

10. The Royal Arch Degree and the "Lost Word"

    a. Attainment of the Royal Arch degree involves the repossession of the "lost word." (According to Masonic history, the Grand Masonic Word was supposed to have been lost during the building of Solomon's Temple.)

    b. Masonic historian Duane Darrah writes: "One of the arguments for the Royal Arch Degree at the present time is that it is necessary in order to complete the Masonic knowledge of the candidate for the reason that the loss of the word in the Master Masons Degree demands that it shall be again found and this is what is accomplished in the Royal Arch Degree."[18]

    c. Rituals in the initiation of Royal Arch Masons include the ceremonial reenactment of the Old Testament captivity of the Jews in Babylon: Royal Arch Masons participate in the struggle, captivity, and subsequent release by Cyrus the Persian monarch.

    d. Many Old Testament Scriptures are used, including Exodus 3:1–6; 2 Chronicles 36:11–20; Ezra 1:1–3; and Psalms 141–143.

---

[18] Duane Darrah, *History and Evolution of Freemasonry* (Chicago: Charles T. Power Co., 1967), 342–43.

e. The candidates are supplied with the necessary tools—a crowbar, pickaxe, and spade—to clear away the rubble around Solomon's Temple.

(1) They then discover the Ark of the Covenant in Solomon's Vault.

(2) They open the vault to find the scroll of the Pentateuch, from which portions are read.

(3) Also included in the symbolic discovery is a pot and Aaron's rod.

f. After more readings and accompanying ceremony, the candidates are now ready to receive the "lost word" ("Jah-Bul-On") following a final reading from John 1:1–5.

(1) Jah represents the Hebrew for "I AM," the Roman Jove, and the Christian Jesus or "Alpha and Omega."

(2) Bul, Bel, or Baal represent the Chaldean and Phoenician chief deity.

(3) On, Eigne, or Aum are the names of the Egyptian and Greek deity.

g. After receiving this "word" the candidates are received as Companion Royal Arch Masons.[19]

h. The significant factor lies in the Royal Arch Masons' ardent belief that their history dates back to the time of Solomon and the subsequent captivity of the Israelites.

11. Oaths Sworn by Royal Arch Masons

a. One version reads: "I will assist a companion Royal Arch Mason when I see him engaged in any difficulty, and will espouse his cause so far as to extricate him from the same, whether he be right or wrong."[20]

b. A more graphic example reads: "To all which I do most solemnly and sincerely promise and swear, with a firm and steadfast resolution to keep and perform the same, without any equivocation, mental reservation, or self-evasion of mind in me whatever; binding myself under no less a penalty than to have my skull smote off, and my brains exposed to the scorching rays of the meridian sun, should I knowingly or willfully violate or transgress any part of this my solemn oath or obligation of a Royal Arch Mason. So help me God and keep me steadfast in the due performance of the same."[21]

---

19 Malcomn C. Duncan, *Masonic Ritual and Monitor* (Chicago: Ezra A. Cook Publishers, 1968), 218–65.

20 Duncan, *Masonic Ritual and Monitor*, 230.

21 Duncan, *Masonic Ritual and Monitor*, 230.

C. The Scottish Rite

1. The Scottish Rite represents the other branch of Freemasonry which a Mason may choose to follow once he has achieved the degree of Master Mason.

2. The Scottish Rite did not come to America via Scotland, but rather from Jamaica via France in 1801.

3. The first Supreme Council was formed in Charleston, South Carolina in 1801.[22]

4. There are four Lodges or Chapters.

   a. The Lodge of Perfection

   b. The Grand Council of the Princes of Jerusalem

   c. The Grand Chapter of Rose-Croix[23]

   d. The Grand Consistories of Divine Princes

5. The Scottish Rite is also known as the "Ancient and Accepted Scottish Rite."

6. There are two requirements for proceeding in the Scottish Rite.

   a. One must be a Master Mason.

   b. One must be a member in good standing in the Blue Lodge.

7. Scottish Rite Freemasonry is the most popular, and is found in every country where the Lodge has established itself.

8. The Scottish Rite confers an additional twenty-nine degrees, in addition to the three degrees conferred by the Blue Lodge.

9. The highest ranking degree is the 33rd. This ranking is called the "Knight Commander" and is conferred by the Supreme Council to its most excellent 32nd degree members.

10. Each of the four Chapters (see C.4. above) confers certain degrees of the Scottish Rite, some of the degrees having pompous titles, such as "Sublime Prince of the Royal Secret," and "Grand Elect Perfect and Sublime Mason."[24]

D. Other Masonic Orders

There are numerous orders within Freemasonry which are derived from the British tradition described above. The following groups are more appendages to the main bodies of Freemasonry.

1. Ancient Arabic Order of the Nobles of the Mystic Shrine (popularly called Shriners).

   a. The Shrine was founded in 1872.

---

[22] Some Masons argue that the first Supreme Council met as early as 1781; see W. G. Sibley, *The Story of Freemasonry* (Gallapolis, Ohio: The Lion's Paw Club, 1904), 69.

[23] There is no historical connection between Rosicrucianism (Ancient Mystical Order of the Rosy Cross—AMORC) and Freemasonry.

[24] For an excellent summary of the mythology surrounding each of these degrees, consult Schmidt, *Fraternal Organizations*, 133–36.

(1) Thirteen Masons met at a restaurant in New York and developed the idea of forming a fraternity where fellow Masons could gather for fun and socializing, apart from the normal ritual gatherings.

(2) Two Americans, Dr. Walter Fleming and actor William Florence, developed the idea.[25] Fleming named the new organization the Ancient Arabic Order of the Nobles of the Mystic Shrine (AAONMS).[26] Fleming played a major role in the early development of the Shrine, including the design of the costumes, head gear, formulation of the symbols, rituals, and emblems (the emblem is the scimitar, upon which is embedded a crescent with the Egyptian Sphinx, and between the two points of the crescent is a five-pointed star).

b. Shriners are composed of York and Scottish Rite Masons who gather strictly for the purpose of "extra-curricular fraternization." In order to become a Shriner, one must have achieved the 32nd degree of the Scottish Rite or the Knights Templar degree of the York Rite.[27]

c. The national leadership of the Shrine comes under the auspices of the "Imperial Council."

d. Since 1922, the Shrine has done outstanding work with children's hospitals and also is known for its famous burn centers.[28]

(1) The Shrine operates three burn institutes in Boston, Massachusetts, Galveston, Texas, and Cincinnati, Ohio. These facilities are staffed with medical professionals and the latest equipment, and are affiliated with the most outstanding medical schools in the country.

(2) Services to patients are free of charge.

2. The Order of the Eastern Star

a. Membership

(1) The Order of the Eastern Star is open to women who are related to Masons, Master Masons, their wives, daughters, legally

---

[25] According to Schmidt, when Florence was in Marseilles, France in 1867, he was invited to a musical comedy where, in the final scene, the actors were made members of a secret society. This proved to be the seed of what would soon become the Shrine ritual.

[26] Note that the letters of "AAONMS" can be rearranged to form the word "Mason."

[27] Concerning the Shrine, H. W. Coil writes: "This is often called the 'Playground of Masonry' and recruits its members from Knights Templar and 32nd degree Scottish Rite Masons, whence the idea has risen that it is a high degree, if not the highest degree of Freemasonry. But it is not a degree and is not and does not pretend to be Masonic; nor do its legends, symbols, or ceremonies resemble those of Freemasonry" (*A Comprehensive View of Freemasonry* [New York: Macoy Publishing and Masonic Supply Co., 1954], 199).

[28] There are twenty-one Shriners Hospitals for Crippled Childrn located throughout the United States, Canada, and Mexico.

adopted daughters, mothers, widows, sisters, half-sisters, granddaughters, stepmothers, and stepsisters.[29]

(2) Requirements for membership include the belief in a Supreme Being, freedom from alcohol addiction, and upstanding moral character.

b. Founded in 1850

(1) Dr. Robert Morris founded the order.[30]

(2) Morris had himself become a Mason only a year earlier in 1849.

(3) He was convinced that the relatives of Masons should be able to participate in the benefits enjoyed by their male counterparts.

(4) In 1855 Morris organized the first order and placed himself at the head with the title, "Most Enlightened Grand Luminary."

c. Disagreement Within the Lodge

(1) Albert Mackey found the idea of women participating in Freemasonry rituals and secrets reprehensible: "When females are told that in receiving these degrees they are admitted to the Masonic Order, and are obtaining Masonic information . . . they are simply deceived. . . . The deception is still gross and inexcusable."[31]

(2) Eventually, the need for an alternative order for women came to be more accepted.

(3) In 1868, Robert Macoy organized a Supreme Grand Chapter and rewrote much of Morris's ritual; the influence of both Macoy and Morris can be seen in the Eastern Star to this day.

d. Five Degrees

(1) There are five degrees in the Eastern Star, based on five women from the Bible.

(2) The leader is called the Worthy Matron, and she, along with the Conductress, assists in the rituals of the Order.

(3) The five women around whom the rituals are based are: Adah (first degree) stressing obedience, Ruth (second degree) stressing devotion, Esther (third degree) stressing fidelity, Martha (fourth degree) stressing faith, Electa (fifth degree) stressing charity.[32]

---

[29] Schmidt, *Fraternal Organizations*, 99.

[30] Although other Masons attempted to date the origins of the Eastern Star as far back as 1775, Morris himself disavowed this precedent, claiming himself to be the sole originator of the organization.

[31] Albert G. Mackey, *Encyclopedia of Freemasonry*, rev. ed., (Chicago: The Masonic History Co., 1946), 32.

[32] The name "Electa" is referenced in 2 John 1. It is Latin for "elect" or "chosen" lady.

e. The Purpose for the Order

"To provide for the welfare of the wives, daughters, mothers, widows, and sisters of Master Masons. Here we may share with the Masonic brother in promulgating the principles of Brotherly Love, Relief, and Truth. Here we may aid, comfort, and protect each other in our journey through the labyrinth of human life, and by cheerful companionship and social enjoyments, lighten the burdens of active duty."[33]

f. The Work of the Eastern Star

Like the Shriners, the Eastern Star operates a number of philanthropic organizations including hospitals, orphanages, and shelters.

3. Daughters of the Eastern Star

a. Organized in 1925

b. Degrees

Daughters of the Eastern Star conferred three degrees called "Initiatory," "Honorary Majority," and "Public."

c. Membership

(1) The Daughters of the Eastern Star was founded for girls ages fourteen to twenty whose fathers were Masons or whose mothers were members of the Eastern Star.

(2) Local groups were called "Triangles."

(3) The organization is found only in New York.[34]

4. The Order of the White Shrine of Jerusalem

a. Organized in Chicago in 1884

b. Membership

(1) The presiding officer is called the Supreme Worthy High Priestess.

(2) The Eastern Star refused to recognize it as a legitimate organization.

c. The headquarters for the order are in Romulus, Michigan.

5. The Order of DeMolay

a. Name

The Order takes its name from Jacques DeMolay, the fourteenth-century leader of the Knights Templar who was burned at the stake.

---

[33] New Rituals, 47–48, taken from "Order of the Rainbow," prepared by Philip Lochhaas, executive secretary: Commission on Organization, the Lutheran Church-Missouri Synod, (n.d.), p. 1.

[34] Alvin Schmidt believes it is difficult to determine whether or not the organization still exists (*Fraternal Organizations*, 97).

b. Founded in 1919

Frank S. Land started the first group with nine high school students from Kansas City, Missouri.

c. Membership

(1) Candidates include white males ages fourteen to twenty-one.

(2) DeMolay is not directly affiliated with any Masonic Lodge, and membership in DeMolay is not automatic.

(3) The Order of DeMolay enjoyed its greatest growth and most widespread popularity during the 1950s–60s.

(4) DeMolay chapters are located throughout the world.

d. Emphasis

DeMolay emphasizes patriotism, citizenship, good morality, cleanliness, and faith in God.

6. The International Order of Job's Daughters

a. Founded in 1920

(1) Job's Daughters was founded by Ethel T. W. Mick in Omaha, Nebraska.

(2) The order, along with Rainbow (see 7. below), are sister orders which are sponsored by the Lodge and Eastern Star.

(3) Mick was a member of the Eastern Star.

b. Purpose

(1) Mick founded the order to give girls between the ages of eleven and twenty an opportunity to develop moral and spiritual character.

(2) Like Eastern Star and Shriners, Job's Daughters participate in philanthropic deeds for the benefit of the community.

(3) A college fund is established for members to borrow from at no cost.

c. Rituals

(1) The ritual of the order is based upon the Book of Job: "Nowhere in all the land were there found women as beautiful as Job's daughters; and their father granted them an inheritance along with their brothers" (Job 42:15).

(2) Secret rituals are enacted which members are sworn not to divulge.

d. Membership

(1) Membership is limited to white females. There are exceptions to this rule in today's IOJD, but the majority of organizations still uphold this principle (concerning racism, see F. below).

(2) Job's Daughters is a worldwide organization and operates on national, regional, and local levels.

7. The International Order of Rainbow for Girls
   a. Founded in 1922
      Rev. Mark Sexson, a chaplain of the Grand Lodge of Oklahoma, founded Rainbow Girls.
   b. Purpose
      The primary purpose is to prepare girls for membership in the Eastern Star.
   c. Membership
      Membership in the order is limited to white girls between the ages of twelve and twenty. (See the section on racism at F. below.)
   d. Organization
      (1) Local chapters are called Assemblies, statewide meetings are Grand Assemblies, and the nationwide organization is called the Supreme Assembly.
      (2) Candidates are recommended by Masons or members of the Eastern Star.
   e. Rituals
      (1) Faith, Hope, and Charity (love) are the basis of the Rainbow ritual.
      (2) Genesis 9 is also alluded to: God makes a covenant not to destroy the earth again by flood, and he seals his promise with the sign of the rainbow.
      (3) As each different order has a varied emphasis, the theme which is used in the initiation is the search for the proverbial pot of gold which lies at the end of the rainbow.
      (4) Seven lessons are provided as the "Sister of Faith" leads the candidate through seven stages in the initiation process. The Bible, colors which have deep symbolism, and an elaborate ritual, are involved in the initiation process and in the regular meetings

8. The Order of Amaranth
   a. History
      (1) Masonic historians trace the origin of the Order's name to 1653 where Christina, Queen of Sweden, desired to form a social organization called "Order of Amarinth." The amaranth is a flower symbolizing eternal life. Having no ties to Freemasonry, the queen's organization comprised fifteen knights and fifteen ladies.[35] Some of the ceremonies that were practiced proved to be influential in American culture in the nineteenth century.

---

[35] It would have been impossible for Christina to have had any ties to Freemasonry, since Freemasonry did not arise until sixty years later.

(2) In 1860, James B. Taylor, an American Mason from New Jersey, began writing a new order based on the Swedish model. Taylor's work served as the catalyst for Robert Macoy and Robert Morris to write rituals, a court system, and a series of degrees in what would become the Order of Amaranth.

(3) The Order was founded in New York City in 1873, with membership open to all Master Masons, their wives, daughters, granddaughters, sisters, widows, etc.

  b. Organization

It is organized into local Courts, Grand Courts (statewide), and an international Supreme Council.

  c. Three degrees

(1) Order of the Eastern Star

(2) Queen of the South

(3) Order of Amaranth

  d. Purpose

The purpose for the Order, as stated in its *Authorized Ritual*, is to be an organization in which one's duties to God, country, and fellow human being are stressed.

  e. Ritual

Ceremonies include frequent usage of the Bible, biblical symbols such as a sword signifying the guarding of the heart against the "wiles of the evil one," and a wreath of Amaranth, symbolizing immortality.

9. Lesser Masonic orders

  a. Daughters of Mokanna

  b. Daughters of the Nile

  c. Knights of the Red Cross

  d. Ladies Oriental Shrine of North America

  e. National Sojourners

  f. Order of the Builder

  g. Social Order of the Beauceant of the World

  h. Tall Ceders of Lebanon of the USA

  i. True Kindred

E. Masonic College Fraternities

1. General Observations

  a. The concept of the college fraternity was born at the College of William and Mary in 1776, though it was not until the twentieth century that fraternities spread to most college campuses across the United States.

    b. Although many fraternities had no connection with the Lodge, many fraternities and sororities adopted rituals and practices used by the Lodge, including

        (1) Mystery

        (2) Secrecy

        (3) Oaths of loyalty

        (4) Grips

        (5) Signs

        (6) Tradition

        (7) Emblems

        (8) Badges

    c. There are several specifically Masonic-affiliated fraternal organizations.

        (1) Acacia

        (2) The Square and Compass

        (3) Sigma Mu Sigma

        (4) The Order of the Golden Key

        (5) Tau Kappa Epsilon

2. Description of Masonic College Fraternities

    a. Acacia

        (1) The term *acacia* means "everlasting life" and was first coined at the University of Michigan.

        (2) According to Coil, the specific purpose was ". . .to distinguish it from Greek-letter fraternities and to associate it with Freemasonry."[36]

        (3) Membership requirements were eased after revisions in 1931, 1933, and 1950. A male student could become a member of Acacia if he were the son or the brother of a Mason, or was recommended by at least two Master Masons (i.e., he himself did not have to be a Mason). These changes were made because fewer and fewer college men were becoming attracted to Freemasonry as the twentieth century progressed, due to various reasons, not the least of which has been that its rituals were beginning to be considered quaint and its membership increasingly comprised older men.

    b. The Square and Compass

        (1) In 1897, on the campus of Washington and Lee University, an organization called the Masonic Club became the forerunner of the Square and Compass, which was formed in 1917. After

---

[36] H. W. Coil, *Coil's Masonic Encyclopedia* (New York: Macoy Publishing and Supply Co., 1961), 14–15.

World War II, the Square and Compass merged with another Masonic fraternity, Sigma Mu Sigma.

(2) Because students who were members of Greek fraternities were not allowed to be members of Acacia, Square and Compass was formed to overcome this obstacle.

(3) Membership was granted through an application process.

c. Sigma Mu Sigma

(1) Sigma Mu Sigma originated on the campus of Tri-State College in Angola, Indiana.

(2) Sigma Mu Sigma was formed by three Knights Templar and nine Master Masons to inculcate the traditions of Freemasonry into college men.

(3) Membership included members of Greek societies.

d. The Order of the Golden Key

(1) Golden Key was formed in 1925, at the University of Oklahoma.

(2) Membership composed of Freemasons, and new members are brought in through invitation.

(3) The rituals are designed to educate young college men so that they might better understand Freemasonry and its initiation rites.

e. Tau Kappa Epsilon

(1) Tau Kappa Epsilon was formed in 1899, at Illinois Wesleyan University.

(2) Originally named Knights of Classic Lore, the name Tau Kappa Epsilon was adopted in 1902.

(3) Virtually identical to Sigma Mu Sigma, it absorbed some of its chapters in 1934.

F. Prince Hall Freemasonry

1. Prince Hall Masonry (black Masons) arose as a result of blacks being barred from membership in the Lodge.

2. In the late 1700s, Prince Hall, a black man from the British West Indies, migrated to America. He served as a pastor for a congregation in Cambridge, Massachusetts.

a. Hall desired to become a Mason; the British Army Lodge accepted him into membership in July 1775.

b. Hall petitioned the Lodge of Massachusetts for membership and was denied because he was black.

c. Hall petitioned the Grand Lodge of England and was granted the desired charter in March 1784.

    d. There is a certain irony here: The English Lodge which recognized Prince Hall Masonry as legitimate was the same Lodge which recognized all of the white Lodges in America. For this reason, many historians have viewed the racism issue as an American phenomenon.

3. Many believe racism no longer exists within the Lodge.

    a. Reasons why this is not true

        (1) No one Lodge can act as an official voice for the entire movement of Freemasonry and, indeed, no one Lodge attempts to do so.

        (2) Each Lodge may follow its own self-imposed guidelines, although the official writings of Masonic scholars are regarded as reliable guidelines to much of current as well as traditional Masonic thought.

        (3) Since blacks have not been permitted to join American Lodges, they have their own Lodges known as Prince Hall. Non-white (black) participants in Freemasonry have formed "clandestine" Masonic Lodges ("clandestine" meaning illegitimate; Prince Hall Masonry is an example of a clandestine Lodge not recognized by conventional Masons). Delmar Darrah said, "Regardless of the way and manner that Negro Freemasonry arose in America, it is spurious and illegitimate."[37]

    b. Attitudes toward blacks have certainly softened, as more blacks have become members of certain Lodges.

G. *Freemasonry and Mormonism*

1. Exclusion of Mormons

    a. While the Lodge accepts all but atheists as members, there is one exception—Mormonism, at least in the Utah Grand Masonic Lodge.

    b. The current code of the Utah Grand Masonic Lodge states: "The Mormon church is an organization, the teachings and regulations of which are incompatible with membership in the Masonic Fraternity. Therefore a member of the Church of Jesus Christ of Latter-day Saints, commonly called the Mormon Church, is not eligible to become a member of any Masonic Lodge in this State, and membership in such Church shall be sufficient grounds for expulsion."

2. Reasons for excluding Mormons

    a. Mormon and Masonic rituals are almost identical.

---

[37] Darrah, *History and Evolution of Freemasonry*, quoted by Schmidt, *Fraternal Organizations*, 123–25.

    b. Mormons and Freemasons both claim to possess the oldest rituals derived from Solomon's Temple and that the other group has a more recent and corrupt version.

    c. Utah Masons do not approve of the polytheism practiced by Mormons.[38]

3. Joseph Smith (1805–1844), the founder of the Mormon Church, was a member of the Mount Moriah Lodge in Palmyra, New York.

4. The Book of Mormon

    a. The Book of Mormon, one of the primary texts for Mormons, mentions secret signs and words, such as one finds in the Masonic ritual.

    b. One example of secret signs states: "And it came to pass that they did have their signs, yea, their secret signs, and their secret words; and this that they might distinguish a brother who had entered into the covenant, that whatsoever wickedness his brother should do he should not be injured by his brother, nor by those who did belong to his band, who had taken this covenant" (Helaman 6:22).

H. Freemasonry and the Southern Baptist Church

In the mid 1980s the Lodge received national attention among Southern Baptists when a resolution questioned Freemasonry's compatibility with Southern Baptist doctrinal tenets. (Many Southern Baptist ministers and laypeople were Lodge members.)

1. The Convention assigned the Home Missions Board (HMB) to study the issue.

2. In 1986, the HMB concluded that "Freemasonry does not fall within the scope of assigned responsibility of HMB," because the Interfaith Witness Department "does not recognize Freemasonry as a religion," and set aside the issue.[39]

3. In 1992, Southern Baptist physician Dr. James Holly charged the Southern Baptists as "the first Christian denomination that essentially blesses the Masonic Lodge."[40]

4. The 1992 Southern Baptist Convention appointed the Interfaith Witness Department of the HMB to study the compatibility of Southern Baptist and Masonic doctrine.

5. In March 1993, the HMB published a report on Freemasonry.

    a. Commendations

        (1) The Lodge's works of charity, education, etc.

---

[38] As will be seen in Part II, Masons are not such strict monotheists as they might claim.

[39] Richard H. Curtis, "Can a Southern Baptist Be a Mason?" *The Northern Light* 24, no. 3 (August 1993): 5.

[40] "Masonry Is Anti-Christian," *Christian News* 32, no. 21 (May 24, 1993): 1.

(2) Those tenets of Freemasonry which are compatible with Christianity (emphasis on honesty, integrity, industry, character)

b. Differences

(1) Offensive titles such as "Worshipful Master"

(2) Bloody oaths and obligations

(3) Pagan and occult nature of many of the writings of past Masons (Pike, Mackey, Wilmhurst, etc.)

(4) The Bible's shared role among other items in the temple

(5) Salvation by works

(6) Universalism (all will be saved) as a teaching prevalent in some Masonic sources

(7) The refusal of most Lodges (although not all) to admit for membership African Americans[41]

c. The Southern Baptist Conclusion

"In light of the fact that many tenets and teachings of Freemasonry are not compatible with Christianity and Southern Baptist doctrine, while others are compatible . . . we therefore recommend that consistent with our denomination's deep convictions regarding the priesthood of the believer and the autonomy of the local church, *membership in a Masonic Order be a matter of personal conscience.* Therefore we exhort Southern Baptists to prayerfully and carefully evaluate Freemasonry in light of the Lordship of Christ, the teachings of the Scripture, and the findings of this report, as lead by the Holy Spirit of God" [emphasis added].[42]

d. Problems with the Southern Baptist Reasoning

The faulty logic of the Southern Baptists becomes apparent when it is applied to other cults.

(1) For example, the Jehovah's Witnesses hold many "tenets and teachings . . . not compatible with Christianity and Southern Baptist doctrine [e.g., denial of the Trinity, deity of Christ, bodily resurrection, etc.], while others are compatible [e.g., belief in the inspiration and inerrancy of Scripture; a personal God; emphasis on honesty, integrity, industry, character; etc.]."

(2) Why, then, don't Southern Baptists allow participation and cooperation with the Witnesses "as a matter of personal conscience" ?

---

[41] Curtis, "Can a Southern Baptist Be a Mason?" 4.

[42] "A Report on Freemasonry," Home Missions Board, Southern Baptist Convention, March 17, 1993. The report was included in the *SBC Book of Reports.* We have used the report as it was reproduced in *Christian News* 31, no. 21 (May 24, 1993): 3.

6. Masonic literature and mailings urged all Southern Baptist Masons to attend the convention in June 1993 as delegates and active participants.

7. At the convention, the Southern Baptists voted to approve the report of the HMB and accept the ruling that membership in the Lodge be a matter of personal conscience, thereby making the Southern Baptist denomination the first among large conservative church bodies to openly accept Masons into church membership.

III. Vital Statistics

A. *Membership Figures*[43]

1. Total Number of Master Masons in the United States Grand Lodges (1924–1991)

   a. In 1924, there were 3,077,161 Master Masons; throughout the 1920s there was steady growth.

   b. However, beginning with the 1930s and through 1945, membership went from 3,279,778 in 1931 to 2,451,301 in 1941.

   c. After World War II, membership increased to 4,103,161 in 1959.

   d. Beginning in 1960, Freemasonry has shown a steady decline in membership in every year up to 1991 and the present.

   e. 1991 membership was reported at 2,452,676.

2. Estimate of the Breakdown (as of 1991 unless noted) of Specific Memberships[44]

   a. The Blue Lodge, also called Symbolic or Craft Masonry: 2,452,676 members

   b. York Rite: 264,484 members

   c. Scottish Rite: 907,720 members

      (1) The Northern Jurisdiction, as of July 1992, has 382,720 members.

      (2) The Southern Jurisdiction, as of July 1992, has 525,000 members.

   d. Shriners: 687,296 members (as of December 1992)

   e. Eastern Star: 20,750 members

   f. Rainbow: 25,000 (approximate membership estimate)

   g. Prince Hall: 2,500 members in Massachusetts[45]

---

[43] The figures quoted here were obtained by directly contacting each of the Lodges. Some figures are accurate as of 1991. Others are rough estimates, since some of the organizations were only able to provide approximate figures.

[44] For updated figures, the reader may contact the Masonic Service Association at: 8120 Fenton Street, Silver Spring, MD 20910–4785.

[45] Total membership figures were unavailable. It would be necessary to contact each state for total membership.

    h. Daughters of the Nile: approximately 70,000 members in the United States and Canada

    i. Order of the Shrine of Jerusalem: approximately 70,000 members in the United States

    j. De Molay: approximately 27,970 members in the United States

    k. Job's Daughters: (current figures are unavailable)

    l. Order of Amaranth: approximately 13,500 members in the United States

B. *Literature Distribution*

1. Each state's Lodges print publications which are distributed to its members, so a rough estimate can be made based upon the membership figures cited above.

2. Some periodicals are sent to members worldwide; a number of these are listed in the bibliography, pp. 61–69.

3. There are also a number of Research Lodges.[46] Several of these are listed in the bibliography section, pp. 69–70.

4. A number of libraries with collections of Masonic literature also exist. Some of these are:

    a. California Grand Lodge Library

    b. San Francisco Scottish Rite Library

    c. Oakland Scottish Rite Library

    d. Colorado Grand Lodge Library

    e. Atlanta Masonic Library

    f. Idaho Grand Lodge Library

    g. Chicago Scottish Rite Library

    h. Indianapolis Scottish Rite Library

    i. Iowa Masonic Library

    j. Library of the Grand Lodge of Massachusetts

    k. Library of the Scottish Rite Supreme Council

    l. Library of the Grand Lodge of Missouri

    m. Scottish Rite Library of St. Louis

    n. Royal Arch Mason's Library in Trenton, Missouri

    o. Nebraska Grand Lodge Library

    p. Grand Lodge of New York Library

---

[46] A Research Lodge is a study center in Freemasonry which studies demographics and statistical information. The addresses of these Lodges are provided in the bibliography.

Part II:
Theology

I. Is Freemasonry a Religion?

A. *Masonic Position(s) on Its Religious Status Briefly Stated*

1. Masonic Authors Who Claim Freemasonry Is a Religion
   a. Albert Mackey
   b. H. W. Coil
   c. Bernard E. Jones
   d. Numerous other sources could be cited, but they tend to be voices from the past.

2. Masons Who Claim Freemasonry Is Not a Religion
   a. Allan D. Large, 32nd degree Mason and Grand Master of the State of Oklahoma, 1991–92
   b. Drs. John E. Jones, 33rd degree Mason and president of Furman University in Greenville, South Carolina, and Basil Manly IV, 33rd degree Mason
   c. R. Stephen Doan, 33rd degree Mason, Grand Master of Masons in California
   d. Rabbi Sidney S. Guthman, 32nd degree
   e. Dr. Norman Vincent Peale, 33rd degree

3. The Majority Position
   a. Today most members of the Lodge insist that Freemasonry is not a religion.
   b. The recent controversy in the Southern Baptist denomination illustrates this position; it was clearly in their best interests to represent the Lodge as a non-religious civic and social organization.

B. *Arguments Used by Masons to Support Their Position on the Religious Status of the Lodge*

1. Masonic Opinion #1: Freemasonry Is a Religion
   a. Albert Mackey states: "There has been a needless expenditure of ingenuity and talent by a large number of Masonic orators and essayists. . . . Freemasonry is . . . an eminently religious organization."[47]

---

[47] Albert G. Mackey, *Encyclopedia of Freemasonry*, 2 vols, rev. ed. (Chicago: Masonic History Co., 1946), 2:847.

b. H. W. Coil

(1) "Freemasonry certainly requires the belief in the existence of, and man's dependence upon, a Supreme Being to whom he is responsible. What can a church add to that except to bring into fellowship those who have like feelings? That is exactly what the Lodge does."[48]

(2) Coil notes that Freemasonry contains a creed, temples, doctrines, altars, worship, and chaplains.

c. Bernard E. Jones

(1) To the argument that there is no recognized ritual, Jones replies: "legal fiction."

(2) Realizing the fact that although no ritual has, in fact, been prescribed by the Grand Lodge, Jones asks whether the "Lodge would soon assert itself, as it has done in the past, if the essentials of the ritual were departed from?"[49]

2. Masonic Opinion #2: Freemasonry Is Not a Religion

a. Allan D. Large

"Religion, as the term is commonly used, implies several things: a plan of salvation or path by which one reaches the afterlife; a theology which attempts to describe the nature of God; and the description of the ways or practices by which a man or woman may seek to communicate with God. Masonry does none of those things. We offer no plan of salvation. . . . Instead, we tell him that he must find the answers to these great questions in his own faith, in his church or synagogue or other house of worship."[50]

b. Drs. John E. Jones and Basil Manly IV

The Lodge is "a fraternity of men, who, first of all, must believe in *one* God. . . . One of the first instructions being given to a member being received into a Masonic Lodge is that Freemasonry will not interfere with his religious or political opinions."[51]

c. R. Stephen Doan

"Religion deals with salvation, the preparation of our spirit for its return to the God who gave it. Masonry, on the other hand, is about ethics: right and wrong conduct in the here and now. . . . Nowhere in our Masonic Ritual is there a promise to our members that they will go to heaven if they are good Masons. Recognized Masonry in this country has never sought to be a means for salvation."[52]

---

[48] Coil, *Coil's Masonic Encylopedia*, n.p.

[49] Bernard E. Jones, *Freemasons' Guide and Compendium* (London: George G. Harrap, 1950), 225.

[50] Allan D. Large, "Questions and Answers on Religion and Freemasonry," *Scottish Rite Journal* (February 1993): 14.

[51] John E. Jones and Basil Manly IV, "Is Freemasonry Compatible with Christianity?" *Scottish Rite Journal* (February 1993): 52.

[52] R. Stephen Doan, "An Open Letter," *Scottish Rite Journal* (February 1993): 42.

d. Rabbi Sidney S. Guthman, 32nd degree

"It is true that Freemasonry believes in a Supreme Deity and in the immortality of the soul and that it has its own ceremonies which it cherishes and reveres. But these points of resemblance to religion are far outweighed by points of difference. Freemasonry does not profess revelation; it has no sacred literature such as the Old Testament, the New Testament, or the Koran; it postulates no dogmas, carries out no sacraments, possesses no seminary or clergy. Furthermore, it has no dietary laws, such as the Jews and Catholics have regulating the food you eat; it has no liturgy or prayers such as the Lord's Prayer of Protestantism, the Ave Maria of Catholicism and the Alenu Lashabeah of Judaism."[53]

e. Dr. Norman Vincent Peale, 33rd degree Mason

"Freemasonry is not a religion, though, in my experience, Masons have predominantly been religious men and for the most part, of the Christian faith. . . . All Masons believe in the Deity without reservation. However, Masonry makes no demands as to how a member thinks of the great Architect of the Universe."[54]

C. Refutation of Masons Who Claim That Masonry Is Not a Religion

1. Disagreement Within the Lodge

   a. Older Masons are less concerned with the hairsplitting distinctions that modern Masons labor under to prove the non-religious status of the Lodge.

   b. Many Masons argue that since Freemasonry recognizes all religions, it itself is not a religion. This argument is untenable (see point 4 below).

2. Definition of *Religion*

   a. Webster's Third *New International Dictionary*

   One of the definitions given for the term *religion* is: "A personal awareness or conviction of the existence of a supreme being or of supernatural powers or influences controlling one's own, humanity's or all nature's destiny."

   b. *Encyclopedia Britannica*

   The fifteenth edition defines *religion* as: "human beings' relation to that which they regard as holy, sacred, spiritual, or divine. Religion is commonly regarded as consisting of a person's relation to God or to gods or spirits. Worship is probably the most basic element of religion, but moral conduct, right belief, and participation in religious institutions are generally also constituent elements of the religious life as practiced by believers and worshipers."

---

[53] Sidney S. Guthman, "Freemasonry a Religion?" *Scottish Rite Journal* (February 1993): 66.

[54] Norman Vincent Peale, "What Freemasonry Means to Me," *Scottish Rite Journal* (February 1993): 40.

3. The Religious Character of the Lodge

   a. That their first principle requires members to be believers in a supernatural deity and bars professing atheists from membership, reveals Freemasonry's fundamental religious predisposition.

   b. Schmidt observes that "the religious qualities of many fraternal societies are also apparent by their rituals. In fact, one might say that the average lodge ritual is very similar to a church's worship agenda in that it commonly includes prayers, pledges, and hymns."[55]

   c. In the Lodge one finds the accoutrements of religion, such as altars, pulpits, readings from sacred literature, etc. Scottish Rite Freemasonry refers to its meeting places as "Temples."

   d. The Lodge speaks of sin, delineates a way of salvation (contrary to Doan's assertion above; see discussion below), describes a personal eschatology (the doctrine of the ultimate destiny of humanity and the world) and has its own prescribed funeral rituals—all of which older Masonic authors readily admit.

   e. Part of the ritual to become a Mason involves being delivered from the pollution of the profane world and receiving "new birth." "There he (the initiate) stands without our portals, on the threshold of this new Masonic life, in darkness, helplessness, and ignorance. Having been wandering amid the errors and covered only with the pollution of the outer and profane world, he comes inquiringly into our doors, seeking the new birth, and asking withdrawal of the veil which conceals divine Truth from his uninitiated sight."[56]

   f. If these Lodge practices are not religious in nature, then one would be hard-pressed to prove that what goes on in a church on Sunday, a synagogue on Saturday, or a mosque on Friday is not actually religious and that the term *religion* is a meaningless concept altogether.

   g. The pen of a Masonic author expresses the truth of the matter: "If the Lodge is not a religion, what would it have to do, that it is not now doing in order to be rightly defined a religion?"[57]

4. "Open-minded" Versus A-religious

   a. It is true that Masonry is open-minded but that is no argument against a religious nature.

   b. For example, Hinduism is an open-minded religion.

      (1) Hinduism teaches that "all paths lead to God."

---

[55] Schmidt, *Fraternal Organizations*, 19.

[56] Albert Mackey, *Masonic Ritualist* (New York: Maynard-Merrill and Co., n.d.), n.p.

[57] Coil, *Coil's Masonic Encyclopedia*, n.p.

(2) Hinduism's tolerance of all religious paths does not negate its religious status. It is therefore illogical to conclude that Free-masonry is not a religious organization simply because it recognizes all faiths.

5. No Comparison with the Boy Scouts

Masons might argue that the Boy Scouts also require belief in God and use the word *reverent* in one of their pledges, yet no one tries to argue that they are a religion. Note the following differences between organizations like the Boy Scouts and the Masonic Lodge:

a. The Boy Scouts do nothing more than include the name "God" in their motto and oaths.

b. The Boy Scouts do not have the accoutrements of religion (see I.C.3.c. above).

c. The Boy Scouts do not try to define sin, a way of salvation, prescribe funeral rituals, etc. (see I.C.3.d. above.).

D. The Biblical Teaching About the Christian Religion and Why Masonry Is Incompatible with It

1. Only One Lord and Savior

a. Being a Christian means trusting only in the work of Jesus Christ on the cross for salvation from sin (John 1:29; 2 Cor. 5:21; Gal. 3:13; Eph. 2:8–9).

b. The very process of joining the Lodge requires Christians to deny everything Christ accomplished on their behalf.

(1) When people become Masons, the initiatory ritual describes them as "in darkness, helplessness, and ignorance. They are said to be "covered with the pollutions of the profane world," "seeking the new birth," and asking for the withdrawal "of the veil which conceals divine Truth from [their] uninitiated sight."[58]

(2) The Bible says that Christians—through faith in Christ—have *already* escaped the defilements of the world (2 Peter 1:3–4), *already* received the new birth (1 Peter 1:22–23), and *already* have the veil of deception removed from their eyes (2 Cor. 4:3–6). Christians—who have *already* received these benefits through Christ—cannot deny that they have them and thus seek them from the Lodge.

2. The Response of the Christian Church to Freemasonry

If the Lodge does not teach matters which are contrary to the Bible, then why do so many denominations forbid membership in the Lodge (the recent position of the Southern Baptist Convention notwithstanding—see Part I, Section II.H.5.d.)?

---

[58] *Masonic Ritualist*, n.p.

a. The Roman Catholic Church

Roman Catholics have historically banned Freemasonry, beginning with the Papal Bull issued by Pope Clement XII in 1738. Eight popes have made official pronouncements against the Lodge, including:

(1) "Freemasonry spreads a system of religious naturalism which not only denies original sin, but which is opposed to all Christian revelation."

(2) "It embraces all the characteristics of a distinct non-Christian religion."

(3) "It requires trivial oaths as serious acts of religious commitment."

(4) "The pantheism of Freemasonry proudly ignores the redemption of mankind, heavenly grace, the sacraments, and eternal happiness and substitutes human reason for Christian revelation."

(5) "It practices blatant racism."[59]

(6) "Its limited morality removed the basis for any ethical system whatsoever."[60]

b. The Eastern Orthodox Church of Greece

This church declares Freemasonry a syncretistic[61] religion which is alien to Christianity.

c. The Rumanian Orthodox Church

This church forbids clerical membership and expects no affiliation of its members.

d. Lutheran Churches

Most Lutheran churches denounced Lodge membership in the nineteenth century. The Lutheran Church Missouri Synod and the Lutheran Church Wisconsin Synod still officially forbid members to affiliate with the Lodge.[62] Further, the LCMS notes that Masonry conducts worship services, has prayers, conducts funeral services, and therefore insists that Masonry is a religion.[63]

e. The Christian Reformed Church

This church denounces the Lodge for its denial that Jesus Christ is the only means of salvation.

---

59 Racism is somewhat toned down in today's Lodges. See the section on racism in Part I, section II.F.

60 Philip Lochhass, *Topic Studies: Christians and Their Affiliations* (St. Louis: Concordia Publishing House, n.d.), 26.

61 Syncretism is the process of "mixing together" Christian teachings with those that are un-Christian in nature.

62 A pamphlet published by the Lutheran Church Missouri Synod entitled *Masonry in Light of the Bible* (St. Louis: Concordia Publishing House, 1954) clearly delineates the denomination's position in this matter.

63 "Masonry Is Anti-Christian," *Christian News* 31, no. 21 (May 24, 1993): 1.

f. The Reformed Presbyterian Church

This church asserts that the Lodge's basic principles are inconsistent with those of Christianity. Further, the Lodge perpetuates ancient mystery religions and this is clearly forbidden to Christians.

g. The Church of God

In 1970 several movements known as the Church of God maintained a posture of complete opposition to Lodge membership.

h. The Orthodox Presbyterian Church

The OPC made it an official position to refuse church membership to Lodge members.

i. The Church of the Nazarene

The Nazarene manual includes a statement which requires its members to not be members of the Lodge.

j. Pentecostals

The various Pentecostal Churches forbid both clergy and laity from Lodge membership. The Assemblies of God (the largest) sets forth a detailed scriptural explanation in its Constitution and By-Laws as to why Lodge membership is forbidden for their members.

k. The Free Methodist and Wesleyan Methodist Churches

The Books of Discipline of both regard Lodge membership as a breach of covenant and in opposition to Christianity.

l. The Mennonite Church

In its "Statement on Christian Fundamentals," The Mennonite General Conference declares that Lodges are "antagonistic to the tenor and spirit of the Gospel." Lodge membership disqualifies one from church membership.

m. Seventh-day Adventists

Adventists forbid Lodge membership because believers are not to be "unequally yoked to unbelievers."

n. The Salvation Army

This denomination opposes Freemasonry on the grounds that the name of Jesus is not given exclusive preeminence in religious ceremonies or services, and "the place where Jesus Christ is not allowed, is no place for any Salvation Army officer."

o. The Quakers

Some Quakers have gone on record denouncing the Lodge for its past discriminatory practices and its requirement for the taking of blood-curdling oaths.

p. Other Churches Which Forbid Membership in the Lodge

(1) The Church of the Brethren

(2) The General Association of Regular Baptist Churches

(3) The Syrian Orthodox Church

       (4) The Ukrainian Orthodox Church

   q. Churches with No Official Position

       (1) The Episcopal Church

       (2) The Greek Orthodox Church

       (3) The United Methodist Church

       (4) The Disciples of Christ.

   r. Other Reasons Why Churches Reject the Lodge

       (1) A deistic concept of God is advanced.

       (2) The Bible is regarded as a mere symbol of truth, instead of the inspired and only Word of God.

       (3) The name of Christ is omitted from prayers.

3. The Lodge's Claims to Be a "Brotherhood"

   The Lodge has stated in numerous periodicals throughout its history that it believes in the "Fatherhood of God and the Brotherhood of Man"—a tenet which is unchristian.

   a. The only basis for asserting that God is "Father," as Jesus taught in the Lord's Prayer (Matt. 6:9–13), is that believers in Jesus are brought into relationship with God as a heavenly parent (Rom. 8:15; Gal. 3:26; 1 John 3:1).

   b. Concerning the "brotherhood of man," the Bible teaches that spiritual unity and solidarity occur only in Christ (John 17:20–21; 1 John 3:1; 4:6), and therefore, the church is the only true Fatherhood and brotherhood.

4. The only proper subject matter of theology, insofar as Christianity is concerned, is Jesus Christ (1 Cor. 2:2).

   a. Masons who speak of an All-Seeing Eye, or the Great Architect in the sky, are speaking of a God that remains hidden from view and therefore is unintelligible.

   b. Christians speak of a specific God who has revealed himself in the person and work of Jesus of Nazareth. If Masons find this narrow and offensive, it only reinforces Jesus' words in John 15:19 (cf. 1 John 3:13).

II. The Bible

A. The Masonic View of the Bible Briefly Stated

1. The Bible is an important book.

2. The Bible is not the exclusive Word of God, nor is it God's sole revelation of himself to humankind, but only one important book among many religious sourcebooks.

3. The source for biblical inspiration is the same as that for all other religious texts, namely, God.

4. The Bible is a good guide for morality.

5. The Bible, together with the "square and compass," are the great lights of Masonry.

6. The Bible is used primarily as a symbol of God's will; God's will can also be captured in other symbolic expressions, such as the sacred texts of other traditions (e.g., the Koran).

B. Arguments Used by the Masons to Support Their Position on the Bible

1. Members must hold to a conviction so long as it is religious in nature.

2. Members must accept the authority of some religious sourcebook.

   a. "The Bible is an indispensable part of the furniture of a Christian Lodge, only because it is the sacred book of the Christian religion. The Hebrew Pentateuch in a Hebrew Lodge, and the Koran in a Mohammedan one. . . ."[64]

   b. "To every Mason, whatever may be his particular religious creed, that revelation of the Deity which is recognized by his religion becomes his trestle board. Thus the trestle board of the Jewish Mason is the Old Testament; of the Christian, the Old and New; of the Mohammedan, the Koran."[65]

3. There is no single, exclusively true, religious sourcebook.

   a. Even if some Masons believe that the Bible is the best sourcebook, being the best does not qualify the Bible for any exclusive claims of authority.

   b. "Whether it be the Gospels to the Christians, the Pentateuch to the Israelites, the Koran to the Muslim, or the Vedas to the Brahman, it everywhere Masonically conveys the same idea—that of the symbolism of the divine will revealed to Man."[66]

   c. Modern Masons who also claim to be Christians are less apt to echo the negative assessment of the Bible made by older Masonic authors. Thus, Judge James B. Wilkinson, Grand Senior Warden of the Grand Lodge in Virginia, writes to Herman Otten, editor of *Christian News*, "The only creed I believe in is the Holy Bible as I have been taught this my entire life. . . . I believe in the Holy Bible. I study it and have a fair knowledge of its teachings."[67]

4. Freemasonry defends its position concerning the Bible based upon its universalist[68] and deistic[69] theological presuppositions.

---

[64] Albert Pike, *Morals and Dogma* (Charleston S.C.: Supreme Council of the 33rd Degree for the Southern Jurisdiction, 1881): 11.

[65] Mackey, *Masonic Ritualist*, 59.

[66] Mackey, *Encyclopedia of Freemasonry*, 104.

[67] Letter reprinted in "Where Do They Stand?" *Christian News* 31, no. 21 (May 24, 1993): 10.

[68] Universalism is the belief that all people are saved no matter what they believe or do not believe.

[69] Deism is basically a rational-critical approach to theism, in which religious beliefs are pared down to a few central tenets (e.g., belief in God, immortality, future rewards and punishments, etc.). It is interesting to note that deism flourished in eighteenth-century England during the years when Freemasonry was also beginning to take root.

C. Refutation of Arguments Used by Masons to Support Their Position on the Bible

1. Christianity does not accept other religious texts.

   a. By accepting the authority of many religious texts, Freemasonry transcends the boundaries of Christianity and the church, which has no other authority but the Bible.

   (1) This is an obvious reason, among others, why virtually every Christian denomination forbids its members from becoming members of the Lodge.

   (2) Virtually every Christian denomination which sets out to examine the teachings of Freemasonry concludes that the Lodge is inherently anti-Christian.

   b. Herein lies a fundamental contradiction for the Mason who claims also to be a Christian: How can one hold to a system which affirms the viability of any religious claim to final authority, and at the same time hold to the Christian faith, which requires its adherents to give exclusive deference to the Bible? (See section II.D. below.)

2. To deny the Bible's exclusive authority is to deny the purpose of Scripture: to communicate what Jesus Christ has done to atone for the sins of the world.

   a. Forrest D. Haggard, a 33rd degree Mason and Christian minister, says: "I have reached a considered decision that Freemasonry is not now and never has been detrimental to my Christian faith and doctrine. In fact my fraternal relationships have strengthened and assisted me in my ministry as well as in my personal faith and life."[70]

   b. In contrast to Haggard's belief, another Masonic writer, Vindex, says: "If true religion is thus to be narrowed down to salvation in no other name under heaven, and St. Paul's words to this effect be understood in a spirit of bigoted literalness, then any such 'Christian' must indeed be straining his conscience to the breaking point by accepting initiation into the broader and deeper mysteries of Freemasonry. I, for one, can never understand how anyone . . . can become a Freemason without suffering from spiritual schizophrenia."[71]

D. Arguments Used to Prove the Biblical Doctrine on the Bible

1. The Bible is the Word of God.

   Christians regard the Bible as the authoritative Word of God; and therefore, the acceptance of other religious sourcebooks runs contrary to the Bible's teaching.

---

[70] Forrest D. Haggard, "A Fraternity Under Fire," *The Northern Light* (February 1990): 12.

[71] Vindex, *Light Invisible* (London: Britons Publishing Co., 1964), 24–27.

    a. Luke 24:44—Concerning the Old Testament Jesus said, "This is what I told you while I was still with you: Everything must be fulfilled that is written about me in the Law of Moses, the Prophets and the Psalms."

      (1) The Old Testament points to Christ.

      (2) Jesus here points to the source of authority which contains all necessary and needful things concerning the Christ.

    b. Luke 16:19–31—In the parable of the rich man and Lazarus, Jesus tells the story of a rich man who dies and goes to hell. There he begs Abraham to send a special revelation to his family on earth so that they will not end up in hell as well. Abraham's response is: "They have Moses and the Prophets; let them listen to them" (v. 29).

      (1) Abraham points to the Word of God, not extra revelations, as the only authority needful for salvation.

      (2) Abraham does not tell the rich man that he need not be concerned about his brothers because they are part of the brotherhood of man and that the all-embracing Fatherhood of God will be sufficient for their souls' salvation.

      (3) Abraham does not tell the rich man that *any* sacred text is sufficient for salvation, as long as people believe in or ascribe to a belief in God.

      (4) Even after requesting a miracle (v. 30), the rich man is denied. "If they do not listen to Moses and the Prophets, they will not be convinced even if someone rises from the dead" (v. 31).

      (5) In other words, the Word of God, as contained in the Bible at that time (the Old Testament), is the exclusive means through which one receives divine revelation needful for salvation.

2. The Bible's contents are not arbitrary, but are in fact God's revelation of himself.

    a. The inspiration of the Old Testament

      (1) 2 Timothy 3:16

      (2) 2 Peter 1:19–21

    b. The inspiration of the New Testament

      (1) 1 Thessalonians 2:13

      (2) 1 Corinthians 2:13

3. The Bible teaches that the only way of salvation is through faith in Christ.

    a. The efficacy of Scripture

      (1) 2 Timothy 3:16

      (3) John 17:17

    b. The sufficiency of Scripture

      (1) No other information from any other religious source is to be relied upon or tolerated.

(2) Galatians 1:6–8—"I am astonished that you are so quickly deserting the one who called you by the grace of Christ and are turning to a different gospel—which is really no gospel at all. Evidently some people are throwing you into confusion and are trying to pervert the gospel of Christ. But even if we or an angel from heaven should preach a gospel other than the one we preached to you, let him be eternally condemned!"

4. The Bible speaks to the issues of *universality* and *particularity*.

   a. Universality

     (1) The Bible, with its saving message (the gospel), is meant by God to be received by *all* people everywhere: "For God so loved the world that he gave his one and only Son" (John 3:16).

     (2) The Bible's message pertains to the whole world (cf. Genesis 17:5–9 with Acts 2:38–39 and 3:24–25).

   b. Particularity

     The Bible communicates a specific message, or a particular revelation, namely, the good news of Christ's sacrificial death on the cross for our sin (see Rom. 3:21–26; John 10:1–18; 14:6; Acts 17:16–31).

   c. Because the Bible's message is both universal and particular, the Bible cannot be a mere alternative for Christians while other texts serve the needs of non-Christian faiths.

   d. The "scandal of particularity" is that no other religion can be correct if Christianity is the truth.

   e. Hence Freemasonry's view of Scripture is erroneous and contradictory from the outset.

III. The Doctrine of God

A. The Masonic View of God Briefly Stated

1. All members must believe in a deity; atheists are denied Lodge membership.

2. Different religions acknowledge the same God.

   a. Along with several of the world religions (Christianity, Judaism, Islam), Freemasonry teaches that there is an eternal being.

   b. However, this God is called by various names.

B. Arguments Used by Masons to Support Their View of God

1. Belief in God is an essential element of Freemasonry.

   a. The *Masonic Ritualist* states: "*A belief in God*—This constitutes the sole creed of a Mason—at least the only creed that he is required to profess"[72] (emphasis added).

---

[72] Mackey, *Masonic Ritualist*, 44.

  b. "Blue Lodge Masonry requires a belief in God but no further religious belief, so that all believers in a deity, whether Christians, Jews, or Mohammedans, are equally eligible for membership."[73]

  c. "Masonry requires only one thing of a man. He must believe in a Supreme Being. No atheist can be a Mason."[74]

2. There are various names for God.

  a. "Therefore it [Freemasonry] invites to its altar men of all faiths, knowing that, if they use different names for 'the Nameless One of a hundred names,' they are yet praying to the one God and Father of all."[75]

  b. Names that Lodge members frequently use when speaking of God are:

    (1) The Supreme Grand Master

    (2) The All-Seeing Eye

    (3) The Supreme Intelligence of the Universe

    (4) The Great Architect of the Universe

C. Refutation of Arguments Used by Masons to Support Their View of God

1. *Which* God one believes in is crucial.

  a. While on the surface it seems commendable and pious to require an aspiring Mason to be a believer in God, the logic of asserting that it does not matter *which* God, deity, name for God, or resulting creed, fails at the outset.

  b. Many of the religions the Lodge seeks to include *themselves* make exclusive claims, asserting that only *their* understanding of God is correct, and thus it is a breach of their faith for these to join the Lodge.

    (1) Islam

    A Muslim daily recites the *Shahada*: "There is no God but Allah, and Mohammed is his prophet."

    (2) Judaism

    To be Jewish is to believe in the one true God: "Hear, O Israel: The LORD our God, the LORD is one" (Deut. 6:4).

    (3) Christianity

    Christianity teaches that the one true God is revealed in the Bible and that Jesus Christ, God incarnate, revealed himself as the only way to God (John 10:1ff.; 14:6; Acts 4:12).

---

[73] *Grand Lodge Proceedings of New Jersey* 23, Part 2 (1908): 95, as quoted in "Freemasonry in Light of the Bible" (St. Louis: Concordia Publishing House, 1954), 12.

[74] Jim Tresner, "Conscience and the Craft: Questions on Religion and Freemasonry," *The Northern Light* 23, no. 1 (February 1993): 18.

[75] *Quarterly Bulletin* (July 1915): 17, as quoted in the pamphlet "Freemasonry in Light of the Bible" (St. Louis: Concordia Publishing House, 1954), 11.

2. While it is not necessarily wrong to refer to or think of God as the "All-Seeing Eye," or "Supreme Intelligence" (Scripture supports both ideas [Prov. 15:3; Ps. 139:1–4]), the Bible reveals many additional names which reveal far more about the nature, personality, and character of God. The very name of the one true God is exclusive of all others by definition (below, D.2.).

   a. Older Masons tend to say that there is only one God who is worshiped under various names (Jehovah, Allah, etc.).

   b. Other Masons indicate that the belief in any deity or deities is a satisfactory fulfillment of the requirement to "believe in God."

3. Freemasonry's doctrine of God is deistic. Lord Edward Herbert of Cherbury (1583–1648), regarded as the father of deism, taught that:

   a. There is a personal creator God who rules the universe.

   b. One is obligated to worship this God.

   c. Virtue and piety are necessary components of worship.

   d. One must repent of his or her sins.

   e. There will be both reward and punishment in the afterlife.[76]

4. Later deists contributed to Freemasonry's plausibility.

   a. M. Tindal (1656–1733) and numerous other British philosophers are included here.

   b. These men eventually paved the way for a fully developed rationalism.[77]

   c. Coupled with a spirit of toleration and optimism, the theological climate changed drastically after the Enlightenment of the eighteenth century.

   d. When Freemasonry came to America, the principles of deism were readily adaptable, thereby paving the way for widespread acceptance.

   e. Freemasonry's doctrine of God closely resembles Lord Herbert's deism.

D. Arguments Used to Prove the Biblical Doctrine of God

1. To be a Christian presupposes the belief in the one true God of Israel (Acts 17:22–31). The bedrock of Judaism and Christianity lies in the teachings of the Old and New Testaments regarding the existence of only one God (Ex. 20:2–3; Deut. 4:35; 6:4; John 4:24).

2. Concerning the name(s) of God, the Bible makes numerous reference to various names and titles.

---

[76] *The Oxford Dictionary of the Christian Church*, ed. F. L. Cross and E. A. Livingstone (Oxford: Oxford University Press, 1983), 638.

[77] Rationalism is the teaching that human reason, as opposed to revelation, is fully capable of knowing whatever can be known. To the rationalist, unaided human reason is the final arbiter of truth.

    a. In the Old Testament, God is most frequently known as *Elohim*, or the Almighty God (Gen 1:1ff.).

    b. The Jewish national name for God is *Jehovah* and is also used frequently in the Old Testament (rendered "sovereign LORD" in NIV— Gen. 15:2; Ex. 6:3; Ezek. 35:3ff.).

    c. *El Shaddai* was used by the Patriarchs to refer to God as the source of comfort and blessing (Ex. 6:3).

    d. *Elyon* is used of the God who is the Most High and is the object of reverence and worship (Gen. 14:18–20).

    e. God appears personally to Moses as the great "I AM" (Ex. 3:14).

    f. In the New Testament God is revealed in the Trinity (see Section IV below), or God the Father, Son, and Holy Spirit (Matt. 28:19; 2 Cor. 13:14).

    g. God is revealed by numerous titles (e.g., the "God of your Father Abraham" [Gen. 26:24], or "the Mighty One of Jacob" [Gen. 49:24]).

3. While Masons will say that even Christians use more than one name for God, each of the names for God fulfill certain criteria:

    a. They refer to the God of Israel.

    b. They refer to the Father of the Lord Jesus Christ.

    c. They reveal something of the nature and personality of the one true God who confronts his people with special and specific revelation about himself.

4. To worship any other gods or to call upon the name of any other deities is regarded as idolatry (Ex. 20:3ff.; 1 Kings 12:25–33; 18:16–40).

    a. This is the sin of many of Israel's kings (1 Kings 12:32; 16:31; 2 Kings 17:12; 21:21; 2 Chron. 25:14; 28:2).

    b. Paul spoke of idolatry as a heinous sin from which the Christian is to flee (1 Cor. 10:14); idolaters will not enter the kingdom of God (1 Cor. 6:9).

    c. John said that idolaters will perish in eternal hell (Rev. 21:8).

IV. The Doctrine of Jesus Christ and the Trinity

A. *The Masonic View of Jesus Christ and the Trinity Briefly Stated*[78]

1. Freemasonry does not allude to God as a divine Trinity, revealed as Father, Son, and Holy Spirit.

2. Because there is no doctrine of the Trinity, there is therefore no doctrine of the deity of Jesus Christ.

---

[78] While fundamental to the structure of Christianity, the doctrine of the Trinity is discussed little in Masonic literature. While non-Christian religions and cults write avidly against God revealed as Father, Son, and Holy Spirit, Masonic literature devotes itself less to this topic than to the general discussion of the existence of God.

3. Freemasonry, except in a few instances, does not incorporate the name of Jesus into its theological writings.
4. Jesus is generally regarded as a great teacher and philosopher, much like Socrates.
   a. Some Masons consider Jesus to be the divine Son of God, in accordance with their own particular piety.
   b. The general practice, however, is to not invoke the name of Jesus when praying, regardless of one's personal belief.

   (1) The concern is that the name of Jesus would offend those non-Christian Masons who are present when prayer is invoked.
   (2) Prayer in the name of Jesus would also create the need to allow the names of Yahweh and Allah to be invoked as well—the kind of religious dispute Masons seek to avoid.
   c. Only in several advanced degrees in which Christianity is brought into focus is prayer in the name of Jesus acceptable.
   d. The same policy holds true for praying in the name of the triune God, Father, Son, and Holy Spirit.

B. *Arguments Used by Masons to Support Their Position on Jesus Christ and the Trinity*
   1. The Trinity
      a. Freemasonry does not affirm the doctrine of the Trinity because to assert such a belief would mark it as a religious organization.
      b. "Masons believe in the light as each individual sees it. To demand belief in a Trinity would be to sponsor a religion. Masonry is not a religion unless striving for the Brotherhood of Man, universal love, and the end of hatred is religion."[79]
   2. Jesus Christ
      a. Jesus Christ stood for virtue in the same tradition and spirit of human brotherhood as other great religious leaders, as evidenced by the following statement: "Truth planted in the hearts of Socrates and Jesus grew and yielded the fruit of noble lives."[80]
      b. Jesus was a teacher of a sublime morality. "If every man were a perfect imitator of the Great, Wise, Good Teacher, Divine or human, inspired, or only a reforming Essene, it must be agreed that his [Jesus'] teachings are far nobler than those of Socrates, Plato, Mohammed, or any of the other great moralists and reformers of the world."[81]
      c. The Masonic view of Jesus Christ reflects its spirit of toleration toward all religions.

---

[79] "An Open Letter to Lutherans Spreading Anti-Masonic Propaganda," *Masonic Inspiration* (Morris Plains, N.J.: Charles Van Cott Publishers, 1958).

[80] *New Age Magazine* (February 1943): 100.

[81] *New Age Magazine* (February 1943): 719.

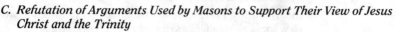

(1) "Toleration, holding that every other man has the same right to his opinion and faith that we have to ours; and liberality, holding as no human being can with certainty say . . . what is truth, or that he is surely in possession of it."[82]

(2) To suggest that Jesus is the only way to God contradicts the principle of toleration.

(3) In answer to the question, *Is Freemasonry "guilty" of teaching toleration?*, 33rd degree Mason, Jim Tresner answers: "Yes. And proud of it! It seems a strange accusation, but anti-Masonic writers often charge that we accept people with many different viewpoints as Brothers. They are correct."[83]

C. Refutation of Arguments Used by Masons to Support Their View of Jesus Christ and the Trinity

1. Those Masons who assert belief in one God must be asked how they know about this God, and does this knowledge contradict other Masonic claims?

   a. One cannot simply claim the belief in God arbitrarily.

      (1) There must be a source of authority.

      (2) If a Mason asserts that he is a Christian, he must also submit to the Bible as his source of authority.

   b. To take the Bible as the definitive source of revealed knowledge about God, one must acknowledge that the Bible makes specific claims about God, such as the triunity of God and the deity of Christ.

   c. Christians believe that God has revealed himself as Father, Son, and Holy Spirit (Matt. 28:19).

      (1) To accept God under the names which other documents or sacred texts use to identify him, is to go beyond how God has revealed himself in the Bible. This is not to say, however, that there are not other names or titles which the Bible itself attributes to God (see Section III.D.2 above).

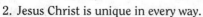

      (2) Christians believe that a saving knowledge of God is available only in the revelation which comes through His word (more in D below).

2. Jesus Christ is unique in every way.

   a. To assert that Jesus and Socrates, or Jesus and any other religious leader, are on the same level, or that Jesus is merely on a higher degree or plane is to contradict Scripture.

   b. Only ignorance or deception can allow a person to deny Christ's uniqueness.

[82] Albert Pike, *Morals and Dogma of the Ancient and Accepted Scottish Rite of Freemasonry* (Richmond, Va.: L. H. Jenkins Inc., 1921), 352.

[83] Jim Tresner, "Conscience and the Craft," *Scottish Rite Journal* (February 1993): 22.

    c. Christ is not different in *degree* but in *kind* from any and all other religious leaders.

      (1) If a Mason is willing to affirm fully and consistently the biblical teaching concerning Christ, then the principles of Freemasonry—which deny the uniqueness of Christ—must be denied.

      (2) On the other hand, if the principles of Christianity are denied, then those of Freemasonry must be affirmed.

      (3) It is logically impossible to simultaneously hold to the principles of Freemasonry and Christianity, especially with respect to the doctrine of Jesus Christ.

      (4) Incorporating Freemasonry and Christianity into one worldview inevitably redefines one, the other, or both.

3. The biblical view of prayer contradicts Freemasonry's view of Jesus.

    a. The name of Jesus is deliberately removed from certain biblical verses used in a number of Masonic writings.[84]

      (1) When 2 Thessalonians 3:6–16 is read in the Royal Arch Degree, the references to Christ in verses 6 and 12 are omitted.

      (2) When 1 Peter 2:3–5 is read at the opening ceremonies of the Mark Master (Fourth) Degree, the words "by Jesus Christ" are omitted. (Mackey refers to the omission as a "slight, but necessary modification" in his *Masonic Ritualist.*)

      (3) For Christians, removing references to Christ from biblical prayers is no "slight modification" but is fundamentally objectionable.

    b. With regard to the very idea of prayer with non-Christians, E. M. Storms says: "For a Christian to stand at an altar believing he is united in prayer with an idol-worshipping pagan suggests one of two things: the Christian is unconvinced of his own message of the Good News of what God has done, or he lacks personal conviction that Jesus Christ is the only way to the Father."[85]

4. Jesus Christ is the *exclusive* and *universal* way of salvation.

    a. Exclusivity

    Christianity claims that Jesus Christ is the *only* way by which fallen humanity may be saved (Acts 4:12).

    b. Universality

      (1) Christ's death and resurrection have implications for the entire world, not just for those whom God calls to faith.

---

[84] The examples listed are noted in Philip H. Lochhass, *Freemasonry in the Light of the Bible* (1954; repr., St. Louis: Concordia Publishing House, 1976), 14.

[85] E. M. Storms, *Should a Christian Be a Mason?* (Fletcher, N.C.: New Puritan Library, 1980), 10.

(2) Jesus is the standard by which all of humankind will be called to account (Phil. 2:9–11).

D. Arguments Used to Prove the Biblical Doctrine of Jesus Christ and the Trinity

1. The only true God is the one who has revealed himself progressively through human history as Father, Son, and Holy Spirit.

   a. God withdrew himself from sinful humanity at the Fall (Gen. 3).

   b. God spoke from that time forth only indirectly through means or instruments:

      (1) The voice of the prophets (OT prophetic books)

      (2) Angels (Luke 1:5–38)

      (3) A burning bush (Ex. 3:1–4)

      (4) The pillars of cloud and fire (Ex. 13:21)

      (5) An audible voice (Ex. 19:9)

      (6) Visions (Ezek. 1)

      (7) Dreams (Dan. 7)

   c. When the incarnation of Jesus Christ took place, God revealed himself directly in the person of Jesus of Nazareth (John 14:9; Heb. 1:1–2).

2. There is no Christianity without Jesus Christ. Masons who claim to be Christians err in supposing that any true religious activity could exclude Jesus Christ and still be a true expression of Christianity.

   a. 1 Corinthians 2:2—Paul demonstrated the centrality of Christ by his obedience to God's call for his life: "For I resolved to know nothing while I was with you except Jesus Christ and him crucified."

   b. John 10:1—Jesus said, "I tell you the truth, the man who does not enter the sheep pen by the gate, but climbs in by some other way, is a thief and a robber."

   c. John 14:6—Concerning the one and only way to God, Jesus declared, "I am the way and the truth and the life. No one comes to the Father except through me."

   d. John 5:23—Those who suppose that they may honor God in ceremonies, worship, and prayer without also honoring the second person of the Trinity should consider Jesus' words: "He who does not honor the Son, does not honor the Father who sent him."

   e. Jesus Christ is a unique person who accomplished a unique work.

      (1) Jesus was God incarnate, God in human form (Matt. 1:18–24; John 1:1; Phil. 2:6; 1 Tim. 3:16).

      (2) As the incarnate Son of God, Jesus is the second person of the Trinity. Although the Bible does not use the word *trinity*, the concept is taught throughout Scripture (Matt. 28:19; Mark 1:9–11; 2 Cor. 13:14).

(3) The biblical teaching concerning the Trinity demonstrates that Jesus is God.

(4) While Masons do not explicitly deny that Jesus is God, by excluding Christ from their prayers and other pious expressions they deny this implicitly.

  f. Jesus fulfilled the threefold office of *Prophet, Priest,* and *King.*

(1) Prophet

Jesus taught and preached the message of the kingdom of God (Deut. 18:15 [cf. Acts 3:22 and 7:37]; Matt. 17:5; Mark 1:14–15; Luke 10:16; John 1:17–18).

(2) Priest

Jesus sacrificed himself for the sins of the world, and now intercedes for his church (Mark 10:45; Gal. 4:4–5; Heb. 7:23–27; 1 John 2:1–2).

(3) King

Jesus rules over all of creation and will one day lead his church on to glory (Matt. 28:18; John 18:36–37; Eph. 1:22; 2 Tim. 4:18).

  g. Jesus was fully *human,* having shared the experiences common to humanity (Phil. 2:5–8).

(1) Grew weary and slept (Mark 4:38)

(2) Felt hunger (Matt. 4:2)

(3) Experienced thirst (John 19:28)

(4) Wept (John 11:35)

(5) Suffered poverty and was persecuted (2 Cor. 8:9; Matt. 8:20; Isa. 53:3; John 8:40, 59)

(6) Was tempted (Luke 4:1–13)

(7) Was severely beaten and crucified (John 19:1–18)

  h. Jesus is also fully *divine,* and as God's Son, he shares all of the attributes of God the Father.

(1) Accorded divine names (John 20:28; Rom. 9:5; 1 John 5:20)

(2) Eternal (John 1:1–2)

(3) Unchanging (Heb. 13:8)

(4) Omnipresent (Matt. 28:20)

(5) Omniscient (John 21:17)

(6) Omnipotent (Matt. 28:18)

(7) Participated in the creation (John 1:1–3; Col. 1:16)

(8) Performed miracles (John 2:1–11)

(9) Forgives sins (Matt. 9:4–8)

(10) Executes divine judgment (John 5:27)

(11) Is worshiped (Heb. 1:6; Phil. 2:9–10; Rev. 5:12–13).[86]

---

[86] The systematic theology presented in this section follows Martin Luther's *Small Catechism* (written by Luther in 1528). The English version used here is the 1943 version (revised 1965) published by Concordia Publishing House.

3. Christians have always prayed in the name of Jesus and the triune God. (See C.3 above on prayer.)

   a. Jesus addressed those who deny or avoid him or his name (including prayer) out of fear of "offending" others.

     (1) Luke 6:26—"Woe to you when all men speak well of you, for this is how their fathers treated the false prophets."

     (2) 1 John 2:23—"No one who denies the Son has the Father."

     (3) Luke 9:26—"If anyone is ashamed of me and my words, the Son of Man will be ashamed of him when he comes in his glory and in the glory of the Father and of the holy angels."

   b. Jesus is to be addressed in prayer, regardless of the possible offense to non-Christians.

     (1) Consciously avoiding the name of Jesus is a form of denial, and "no one who denies the Son has the Father" (1 John 2:23).

     (2) The apostles boldly preached, taught, and performed miracles *in the name of Jesus Christ*, and frequently received opposition for doing so (Acts 4:18–20; 2 Cor. 4:7–11; 6:4–10).

V. The Doctrine of Human Nature and Sin

A. The Masonic View of Human Nature and Sin Briefly Stated

1. Human beings are able to improve their character and behavior in various ways, including acts of charity, moral living, and the voluntary performance of civic duties.

2. Humanity possesses the capability of moving from imperfection toward total perfection.

3. This moral and spiritual perfection lies within men and women, not outside of them, and may be discovered through education.

4. Freemasonry provides the means through which one may achieve these desired results.

B. Arguments Used by Masons to Support Their View of Human Nature and Sin

1. Participation in Freemasonry facilitates moral improvement.

   a. Albert Mackey described progress as being like a ladder.

     "The ladder is a symbol of progress . . . its three principal rounds, representing Faith, Hope, and Charity, present us with the means of advancing from earth to heaven, from death to life—from mortality to immortality. Hence its floor is placed on the ground floor of the Lodge, which is typical of the world, and its top rests on the covering of the Lodge, which is symbolic of heaven."[87]

---

[87] Mackey, *Encyclopedia of Freemasonry*, 361.

b. Ted Lilley, 33rd degree Mason, affirms the moral value of Lodge membership.

"It is very important that we are able to let our friends know that Masons have neither horns, tails, nor halos. We're just their friends and neighbors, joined together in a fraternity which tries to help men become better people as it tries to help the world become a better place through its charities. Freemasonry is a support group, so to speak, for men who are trying to practice ethics and morality in a world that does not always encourage those ideals."[88]

c. Christen Haffner states:

"Within their lodges, Freemasons are not concerned with salvation and conversion, but with taking men as they are and pointing them in the direction of brotherhood and moral improvement."

2. Human nature is not depraved.

a. Robert Macoy

"Nor does Masonry teach that human nature is a depraved thing, like the ruin of a once proud building. Many think that man was once a perfect being but that through some unimaginable moral catastrophe he became corrupt into the last moral fiber of his being, so that, without some kind of supernatural or miraculous help from outside him he can never of himself do, or say, or think, or be ought but that which is deformed, vile, and hideous."[89]

b. Norman Vincent Peale

"Why am I a Freemason? Simply because I am proud to be a man who wants to keep the moral standards of life at a high level and leave something behind so others will benefit. Only as I, personally, become better, can I help others do the same."[90]

3. Men and women can attain moral perfection.

a. "The perfection is already within. All that is required is to remove the roughness, the excrescences, divesting our hearts and consciences of all vices and superfluities of life to show forth the perfect man and Mason within. Thus the gavel becomes also the symbol of personal power."[91]

b. "Man also contains within him a life-force, a 'vital and immortal Principle' as Masonry calls it, which has not yet expanded to full development in him, and indeed in many men is not active at all. Man too, has that in him enabling him to evolve from the stage of the mortal animal to a being immortal, super-human, godlike. . . . Human evolution can be accelerated if not at present in the mass

---

[88] Tresner, "Conscience and the Craft: Questions on Religion and Freemasonry," 19.

[89] H. L. Haywood, *The Great Teachings of Masonry* (Richmond, Va.: Macoy Publishers and Supply Co., 1971), 138–39.

[90] Peale, "What Freemasonry Means to Me," 41.

[91] Carl H. Claudy, *Little Masonic Library* 4 (Richmond, Va.: Macoy Publishers and Supply Co., 1946), 51.

of humanity, yet in suitable individuals. Human nature is per-fectible by an intensive process of purification and initiation."[92]

   c. The gavel, a key symbol of humanity's ability to move toward a state of perfection, represents personal power in Masonic ritual.

C. Refutation of Arguments Used by Masons to Support Their View of Human Nature and Sin

1. Experience shows that human beings (apart from Christ) are not moving toward spiritual perfection.

   a. A Lesson from History

      (1) The Masons' claims of human perfectibility simply do not square with the real world: When faced with choices, people have always been generally selfish by nature.

      (2) The twentieth century has been an era of astounding progress in terms of human knowledge and scientific and technological advancement. Yet, despite the explosion of knowledge, hu-manity is no closer to solving the social, economic, spiritual, and psychological ills which have always plagued it.

      (3) Problems throughout human history include: alcohol and drug abuse, loneliness, depression, murder, theft, divorce, cult involvement, fear, anxiety, confusion, uncertainty, unhappi-ness, etc.

      (4) Masons might argue that this is all the more reason why the world needs more Masons. Nevertheless, the radical sinfulness of the human race is an irrefutable fact of history that hardly squares with Masonry's optimistic view of mankind.

   b. The Bankruptcy of the Lodge

      (1) The Lodge cannot aid human nature in curing humanity of its social ills.

      (2) Masons might argue that the church manifests the same prob-lems (such as Christians who are racists).

      (3) This is correct, but this is also precisely what the Bible says about human nature (see C.2. and D below).

2. Christianity has always maintained that perfection in this life is un-attainable.[93]

   a. Perfection awaits the "blessed hope" of the church, namely, the second coming of Jesus Christ.

      (1) 1 Thessalonians 5:23

      (2) Titus 2:11–13

      (3) 1 John 3:1–3

---

[92] W. L. Wilmhurst, *The Masonic Initiation* (London: John M. Watkins, 1957), 27–28.

[93] Note that even those Christian sects that teach that a kind of perfection is attainable in this life (e.g., Wesleyanism) base their attainment on the work of Christ and the power of the Holy Spirit in the believer.

b. Only Christianity accounts for the origin of sin (the Fall) and its true cure (forgiveness through faith in Jesus Christ).

c. The evening news graphically illustrates the Bible's testimony that humanity is depraved and in itself hopeless.

D. *Arguments Used to Prove the Biblical Doctrine of Human Nature and Sin*

1. The Bible states that sin has affected every human being born into the world.

   a. Romans 3:23—"All have sinned and fall short of the glory of God."

   b. Romans 5:12—"Sin entered the world through one man [Adam], and death through sin, and in this way death came to all men, because all sinned."

   c. See also Genesis 6:5; 8:21; Psalm 51:5; Romans 7:18; 8:7–8; Ephesians 2:1.

2. The Bible denies that humanity, since the Fall, has within itself the capacity for moral perfection.

   a. 1 John 1:8—"If we claim to be without sin, we deceive ourselves and the truth is not in us."

   b. Romans 3:23—"For all have sinned and fall short of the glory of God."

      (1) The use of the present tense shows that all people *presently* and *continuously* fall short of God's standard of absolute moral perfection.

      (2) In the Greek language, the present tense often denotes ongoing action.

   c. If people could be morally perfect through their own efforts they would not need Christ or his work of atonement for sin, but this is not the case.

      (1) In Romans 1:18–25, Paul describes the true condition of human nature (apart from Christ) as being corrupt, vile, and wicked.

      (2) These are hardly attributes that will qualify humanity for godhood.

VI. Oaths

A. *The Masonic Position on Oaths and Symbols Briefly Stated*

1. Oaths and symbols are part of Masonic ceremonies and rites.

2. Oaths are generally regarded as purely symbolic, and therefore, a Mason who is a Christian may make such oaths without a violation of conscience.

B. *Arguments Used by Masons to Support Their Position on Oaths and Symbols*

1. In Defense of the Use of Oaths in the Lodge

"Some religious critics allege that Masons swear oaths on the Bible with penalties which they do not intend to enforce and therefore commit blasphemy. Any thoughtful Mason knows that these penalties are symbolic only. Religions are rich with symbolism also."[94]

2. Concerning Whether a Christian May Take Masonic Vows or Oaths

"Yes, with the exception of a very few denominations. . . . Any Christian whose denomination does not forbid the presidential or the court oath, or the oath taken when entering the Armed Services, could take the Masonic obligations. Some anti-Masonic writers have complained about the so-called "penalties" in the Masonic obligations. Those penalties are purely symbolic and refer to the pain, despair, and horror which any honest man should feel at the thought that he had violated his sworn word."[95]

3. Concerning Symbols

"Masonry uses many symbols—it's our primary way of teaching, as it has been the primary way of teaching from ancient times (just try teaching arithmetic without number symbols), but there is nothing satanic about them. Symbols mean what the person uses them to mean. X may be a St. Andrew's Cross, ancient symbol of Scotland, or it may mean 'multiply two numbers together,' or '10' in Roman numerals. . . . The meaning of the symbol X depends on the symbol's meaning in the mind of the person using it. It is the same with Masonic symbols. We sometimes use the five-pointed star, for example."[96]

C. Refutation of Arguments Used by Masons to Support Their Position on Oaths and Symbols

1. The *fact* that Masons take oaths is not in itself wrong; oaths or pledges are an important part of life.

2. It is the *content* of the oath which is of concern.

   a. A Christian may never take an oath to kill people or to harm them in any way.

   b. Nor may a Christian take an oath to wish to see them harmed *in the name of God.*

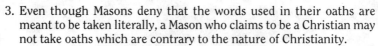

3. Even though Masons deny that the words used in their oaths are meant to be taken literally, a Mason who claims to be a Christian may not take oaths which are contrary to the nature of Christianity.

   a. Masonic oaths are immoral.

   Professor Kurt Marquart of Concordia Seminary says,

   "The dreadful oaths of Masonry are immoral from the Christian point of view not only because of the macabre punishments invoked ('your throat cut across, your tongue torn out by the root,' etc.) in the name of God, but also because it is sinful to swear in

---

[94] Doan, "An Open Letter," 43.

[95] Tresner, "Conscience and the Craft," 21.

[96] Ibid.

UNCERTAIN matters. For the oaths are required BEFORE the candidate discovers the 'secrets.' "[97]

b. Masonic oaths are either idolatrous or blasphemous.

Marquart points out the serious problem which crops up for the "Christian" Mason:

"Either the oaths are taken seriously, but then they are blasphemous (cursing and swearing by God's name). Or else they are not taken seriously, but then they are also blasphemous (literally taking the name of the Lord in vain)! This reflects the general dilemma of Freemasonry: Either it is taken seriously, but then it is a sin against the First Commandment (Idolatry), or else it is not taken seriously, but then is a sin against the Second Commandment (Blasphemy, taking the name of the Lord in vain)."[98]

D. Arguments Used to Prove the Biblical Position on Oaths and Symbols

1. Oaths in God's Name

   The third commandment is: "You shall not misuse the name of the Lord your God" (Ex. 20:7; cf. Lev. 19:12).

2. Cursing

   "With the tongue we praise our Lord and Father, and with it we curse men, who have been made in God's likeness. Out of the same mouth come praise and cursing. My brothers, this should not be" (James 3:9–10; cf. Matt. 5:33–37; 14:6–9; 26:69–75; Acts 23:12).

3. Other Serious Incompatibilities

   a. Masons will have more in common with fellow non-Christian Masons simply because they share the loyalties of the Order.

   b. Jesus condemned divided loyalties in his disciples (Matt. 6:24; 10:37).

---

[97] Kurt Marquart, "Christianity and Freemasonry," *Christian News* (March 19, 1968; rep. May 24, 1993): 23.

[98] Marquart, "Christianity and Freemasonry," 23.

# Part III: Witnessing Tips

A. *Know why people become Masons.*

    1. In order to effectively witness to Masons, it is important to realize why people join the Lodge and become Freemasons, members of Eastern Star, etc.

    2. The Lodge membership appeals to different people for different reasons.

        a. A sense of identity and of belonging

        b. Opportunities for advancement in rank, titles, and office, and for achievement in general

        c. The chance to meet people who share many of the same values and goals (People who share the same interests and values are easily bonded to one another.)

        d. Because Lodge membership affords them certain "advantages" and positive influences in business activities, and though personal ambition may be discouraged in Freemasonry, this motive cannot be overlooked.

        e. Because Freemasonry is known for its commitment to charitable causes

        f. Fascination with secret oaths, wearing costumes, and carrying a sword; that is, participation in the pomp and pageantry

        g. The sense of power that one is afforded when higher degrees and rankings are acheived

        h. Involvement with an organization which advances a religiosity expressed in moral precepts and ornate rituals (Some members find in Freemasonry a religious commitment that becomes a substitute for more conventional forms.)

    3. Knowing why they joined the Lodge will enable you to know how best to direct the conversation toward the truths of Scripture and the fact that all of their deepest needs are ultimately fulfilled in Jesus Christ.

B. *Focus on Christ and salvation by grace.*

    1. When witnessing to a Mason, be prepared to steer the conversation toward Jesus Christ and justification by grace through faith.

2. Many Masons believe that their good works count toward their salvation.

   a. It may prove more engaging to tell Masons that their good works can never earn God's favor and then to show them from the Bible why this is so.

   b. It may also cause some tense moments, but remember that you are declaring the truth (John 14:6), and the truth frequently causes controversy.

3. It is important to point out to Masons that all have sinned and that the human race stands condemned before God.

   a. Masons are often involved in religious activities and are closely associated with the church.

   b. They may respond by saying that God will surely reward their good deeds.

   c. This is an opportunity to point to passages such as Romans 3:23 and 6:23 that teach how ALL have sinned and that the punishment for sin is death.

   d. Then continue with the message of the forgiveness of sins through faith in Christ.

C. *Stick to the important issues.*

Do not get side-tracked by hair-splitting issues that have no real bearing on the matter at hand, but focus on Christ's free offer of salvation to sinners who repent.

D. *Address the issue of "hypocrites" in the church.*

1. Often Masons will point out that many professing Christians are hypocrites because they do not reflect Christ in the way they live. While the institutional church has failed, Masons argue, the Lodge is a divine institution or the true "steward of the mysteries of God" (1 Cor. 4:1 KJV).

2. Agree that there are hypocrites in the church.

   a. There have always been hypocrites, and this will continue until Jesus returns to purify his church and separates true believers from unbelievers (Matt. 13:24–30).

   b. If there were no hypocrites in the church, then Jesus' words would not be true and he would be a liar.

E. *Emphasize the importance of sound doctrine.*

1. The Trend Away from Doctrine

   a. The church in the late twentieth century places increasingly less emphasis on orthodox Christian teaching.

   b. Instead, greater emphasis is placed on personal piety and holiness of life.

    c. Holiness flows *out of* sound doctrine; without doctrine, there can be no growth in Christian character.

    d. God's truth produces his character because he is revealed in his Word.

2. Opposing Worldviews

    a. Christians who join movements like the Masons are usually ignorant of doctrine and therefore unaware of the contradiction between Christianity and Freemasonry.

      (1) To be a Christian means to follow Christ.

      (2) To be a Mason means to follow the religion of choice.

    b. You do well to point out this confusion of worldviews.

3. The Role of the Holy Spirit

    a. Do not expect a person to be persuaded by appealing just to logic or common sense.

    b. A person receives the truths of the Christian faith through the illumination of the Holy Spirit: "The man without the Spirit does not accept the things that come from the Spirit of God, for they are foolishness to him and he cannot understand them, because they are spiritually discerned (1 Cor. 2:14).

F. Remember that Masons are involved in charitable causes and civic and community affairs.

1. Recognize that, though these works do not contribute to one's salvation, the world esteems them and they are very beneficial to the community.

2. Commend Masons for the ways they have served society by their many and varied contributions.

G. Discuss topics of interest to Masons.

1. The Bible

    a. Be prepared to discuss the Bible as the only infallible Word of God upon which the Christian faith places final authority in all matters of faith and doctrine.

    b. See 2 Timothy 3:16–17; John 10:35; 2 Thessalonians 2:15; 1 Corinthians 14:37; 2 Corinthians 13:3; 2 Peter 1:20–21.

2. God

    a. Focus particularly on the Christian belief in one true God.

    b. See Deuteronomy 6:4; 4:35; John 4:24.

3. Human Nature

    a. Point out that human beings are sinners before God and are in no condition to save themselves by their good works: civic involvement, moral rectitude, or exercises in self improvement.

    b. See Psalm 51:1–5; Romans 1:18–32; 3:23; 5:12.

4. Salvation

    a. Affirm that salvation is achieved by faith in what Christ has accomplished on the cross, and that good works are the *evidence* (not the means) of faith.

    b. See Romans 3:28; 6:23; John 3:16–18; Ephesians 2:8–10; Philippians 3:7–9.

5. Sexism

    a. Assert specifically, that God and Christianity have never endorsed the notion that men enjoy any degree of special or superior status.

    b. See Galatians 3:28–29.

    c. Luke 23:27–30—Jesus consoled the women who remained at the scene of the crucifixion.

    d. Matthew 28:1–10; John 20:10–18—After his resurrection, Christ appeared first to women.

II. Approaches to Avoid/Common Mistakes Christians Make

A. False Assumptions

1. "Witnessing to Masons is easy."

    a. Don't assume that witnessing to Masons will be an easy task.

      (1) Masons already consider themselves to be "religious." Masons must subscribe to the belief in some deity.

      (2) People who practice religion, even at a nominal level, usually consider themselves to be in good standing with "the man upstairs."

2. "Masons are impervious to the gospel."

    a. Do not let a psychological barrier deter you from talking about the gospel with Masons, "for God did not give us a spirit of timidity, but a spirit of power, of love and of self discipline" (2 Tim. 1:7).

    b. There is no group of people that is not able to be reached with the Gospel.

3. "Masons are going to hell simply because they are Masons."

    a. Don't assume or tell Masons that they are going to hell or are under the judgment of God simply because they are Masons.

    b. This approach will immediately close off any opportunity for continued conversation because you will be perceived as a closed-minded religious fanatic.

    c. This is not to say that Masons are *not* going to hell, but that they are not going simply *because they are Masons.*

(1) A person goes to hell because he or she denies Christ (Matt. 10:28–33).

(2) As has been observed in Part II, Lodge teachings directly or indirectly deny Christ.

B. Unhelpful Behaviors

1. Do not pretend to be an expert about Masonry if you are not.

   a. Some Christians try to give the impression that they know everything about Masonry when discussing the gospel with Masons.

   (1) This can be an immediate "red-flag" to Masons.

   (2) Wary individuals can quickly discern phony people from sincere ones.

   b. Be humble as you listen to what they have to say, and they may be more inclined to listen to what you have to say.

   c. Do not pretend to know something you do not. If a Mason asks you a question, or points out something you do not know, tell him that you will do some research to find out the answer.

2. Do not be arrogant.

   a. You will not convince Masons of their need to repent of their sin and believe in Jesus Christ for salvation if you haughtily despise what they believe.

   b. A proud or arrogant attitude may convince Masons, or any others for that matter, that what you believe really hasn't done much to improve your character, and that their belief system is better.

   c. The Bible commands believers to be humble and respectful towards unbelievers. "Always be prepared to give an answer to everyone who asks you to give the reason for the hope that you have. But do this with gentleness and respect, keeping a clear conscience, so that those who speak maliciously against your good behavior in Christ may be ashamed of their slander" (1 Peter 3:15–16).

 **Part IV:**
Selected Bibliography

I. Primary Sources

A. Books

Bell, F. A. *The Order of the Eastern Star.* Chicago: Ezra A. Cook Publications, 1956.

Bell presents a brief history of the Eastern Star and its rituals.

Blanchard, J. *Scottish Rite Masonry Illustrated.* Chicago: Ezra A. Cook Publications, 1953.

Cass, Donna A. *Negro Freemasonry and Segregation.* Chicago: Ezra A. Cook Publications, 1957.

Cerza, Alphonse. *Anti-Masonry.* Missouri Lodge of Research, 1962.

Cerza is an avid apologist for the Masonic cause in this work.

Claudy, Carl H. *Introduction to Freemasonry.* Washington, D.C.: The Temple Publishers, 1931.

Claudy provides some helpful comments and insights into Masonic rituals.

_____. *Foreign Countries: A Gateway to the Interpretation and Development of Certain Symbols of Freemasonry.* Richmond, Va.: Macoy Publishing and Masonic Supply Co., 1971.

Clausen, Henry C. *Beyond the Ordinary: Toward a Better, Wiser, and Happier World.* Washington, D.C.: The Supreme Council, 33rd Degree, Ancient and Accepted Scottish Rite of Freemasonry, 1983.

_____. *Clausen's Commentary on Morals and Dogma.* Washington, D.C.: The Supreme Council, 33rd Degree, Ancient and Accepted Scottish Rite of Freemasonry, Southern Jurisdiction of the United States, 1976.

_____. *Practice and Procedures for the Scottish Rite.* Washington, D.C.: The Supreme Council, 33rd Degree, Ancient and Accepted Scottish Rite Freemasonry, Mother Jurisdiction of the World, 1981.

Coil, H. W. *A Comprehensive View of Freemasonry.* New York: Macoy Publishing and Masonic Supply Co., 1954.

Old, but still the definitive source on what constitutes the essence of Freemasonry.

_____. *Freemasonry Through Six Centuries.* 2 vols. Fulton, Mo.: Missouri Lodge of Research, 1966–67.

A helpful and comprehensive view of the history of Freemasonry from the fifteenth century to the twentieth.

_____. *Coil's Masonic Encyclopedia.* New York: Macoy Publishing and Masonic Supply Co., 1961.

Darrah, Delmar Duane. *History and Evolution of Freemasonry.* Chicago: Charles T. Power Co., 1967.

A good account of the true origins of Freemasonry as well as of spurious accounts.

Denslow, Ray Vaughn. *Territorial Masonry.* Kingsport, Tenn.: Southern Publishers Inc., Masonic Publications Division, 1925.

An old, but still good and readable explanation of the history of Freemasonry's growth during the westward expansion.

_____. *Freemasonry Among the Indians.* Fulton, Mo.: Missouri Lodge of Research, 1957.

_____. *Freemasonry and the Presidency, U.S.A.* Fulton, Mo.: Missouri Lodge of Research, 1952.

Tells the story of both Jefferson and Madison's open and active practice of Freemasonry.

Duncan, Malcomn C. *Masonic Ritual and Monitor.* Chicago: Ezra A. Cook Publications, 1977.

A newer edition of the 1946 publication, Duncan provides a readable and accurate history of Freemasonry. The work includes photos.

Haggard, Forest D. *The Clergy and the Craft.* Fulton, Mo.: Missouri Lodge of Research, 1970.

Hammond, William E. *What Masonry Means.* New York: Macoy Publishing and Supply Co., 1939.

A helpful work for understanding Masonic symbols.

Haywood, Harry L. *Freemasonry and Roman Catholicism.* Chicago: Masonic History Co., 1943.

Not intending to be polemical, the author discusses the attitude of the Roman Church toward Freemasonry.

_____. *Famous Masons.* Richmond, Va.: Macoy Publishing and Supply Co., 1971.

_____. *The Great Teachings of Masonry.* Rev. ed. Richmond, Va.: Macoy Publishing and Masonic Supply Co., 1986.

_____. *Newly Made Mason: What He and Every Mason Should Know About Freemasonry.* Richmond, Va.: Macoy Publishing and Masonic Supply Co., 1973.

Henderson, Kent. *Masonic World Guide.* Richmond, Va.: Macoy Publishing and Masonic Supply Co., 1984.

Hunter, C. Bruce. *Masonic Dictionary.* Richmond, Va.: Macoy Publishing and Masonic Supply Co., 1989.

_____. *Beneath the Stone.* Richmond, Va.: Macoy Publishing and Masonic Supply Co., 1992.

Hunter proposes that the Masonic craft originated when the Knights Templar united with earlier stonemasons.

Lanier, John J. *Masonry and Protestantism.* New York: Macoy Publishing and Masonic Supply Co., 1923.

Lanier represents the sentiment common to many Masons that Roman Catholicism is an enemy of democracy.

Mackey, Albert G. *Encyclopedia of Freemasonry.* Rev. ed. Chicago: Masonic History Co., 1946.

One of the most respected of Masonic scholars, Mackey presents a thorough account of Masonic thought and history in this revised version, updated from its original publication in 1887.

_____. *The Manual of the Lodge.* New York: Clark Maynard, 1870.

_____. *Jurisprudence of Freemasonry.* Reprint. Chicago: Charles T. Power Co., 1967.

Mackey elaborates on the various customs, rites, and rules employed in Freemasonry.

_____. *The History of Freemasonry: Its Legends and Traditions, Its Chronological History with the History of the Symbolism.* New York: Masonic History Co., 1905.

_____. *Symbolism of Freemasonry.* Reprint. Chicago: Masonic History Co., 1945.

Macoy, Robert. *Masonic Burial Services with General Instructions.* Chicago: Ezra A. Cook Publications, 1954.

Newton, Joseph Fort. *The Religion of Masonry.* Richmond, Va.: Macoy Publishing and Masonic Supply Co., 1927.

Pike, Albert. *Morals and Dogma.* Charleston, S.C.: Supreme Council of the 33rd Degree for the Southern Jurisdiction, 1881.

Rebold, Emmanuel. *A General History of Freemasonry in Europe.* Cincinnati: American Masonic Publishing Association, 1927.

Robinson, John J. *A Pilgrim's Path: One Man's Road to the Masonic Temple.* Silver Spring, Md.: Masonic Service Association, 1993.

Robinson proves to be a friendly outsider as he seeks to defend Freemasonry from the attacks of not-so-friendly outsiders.

Roth, Philip A. *Masonry in the Formation of Our Government, 1761–1799.* Milwaukee: Masonic Service Bureau, 1927.

Steinmetz, George H. *The Royal Arch: Its Hidden Meaning.* Richmond, Va.: Macoy Publishing and Masonic Supply Co., 1989.

Tatsch, J. Hugo. *Freemasonry in the Thirteen Colonies.* New York: Macoy Publishing and Masonic Supply Co., 1929.

This work draws heavily from Mackey's work and only alludes to the anti-Masonic movement in America.

Williamson, Harry A. *The Prince Hall Primer.* Chicago: Ezra A. Cook Publishers, 1957.

Wilmhurst, W. L. *The Masonic Initiation.* London: John M. Watkins, 1957.

B. Periodicals

Little Masonic Library

Baird, George W. "Great American Masons." *Little Masonic Library* 4 (1946): 93–167.

Barry, John W. "Masonry and the Flag." *Little Masonic Library* 3 (1946): 93–167.

Claudy, Carl H. "A Master's Wage." *Little Masonic Library* 4 (1946): 1–89.

Goodwin, S. H. "Mormonism and Masonry." *Little Masonic Library* 2 (1946): 251–336.

The author compares Mormonism and Freemasonry, demonstrating their incompatibility.

Newton, Joseph Fort. "The Great Light in Masonry." *Little Masonic Library* 3 (1946): 151–206.

Newton shows how the Bible can be used to defend and legitimize Freemasonry.

_____. "The Degrees of Masonry." *Little Masonic Library* 4 (1946): 171–252.

Provides explanations for the various symbols which are used in the degrees of Freemasonry.

Other

Boyden, William L. "Jefferson and Madison Were Masons." *The New Age* 40 (October 1932): 605–6, 612.

Boyden makes the case that at least fifteen U.S. presidents were Masons.

Curtis, Richard A. "Can a Christian Be a Mason?" *The Northern Light* 24, no. 3 (August 1993): 4–6.

Doan, R. Stephen. "An Open Letter." *Scottish Rite Journal* (February 1993): 42–44.

This is a recent attempt to refute Christian critics of Masonry.

Early, Jack J. "Religion and Freemasonry." *Scottish Rite Journal* (February 1993): 26–28.

Early discusses how Christianity and Freemasonry are compatible.

"The Future Relationship Between Freemasonry and the Church: An Educational Problem." *The Short Talks Bulletin* 40, no. 9 (September 1962).

Guthman, Rabbi Sidney S. "Freemasonry a Religion? How Wrong Can You Be?" *Scottish Rite Journal* (February 1993): 66–68.

A rabbi takes on the question of whether the Lodge should be classified as a religion.

Haggard, Forest D. "A Fraternity Under Fire." *The Northern Light* (February 1990): 12.

Haggard, a 33rd degree Mason and pastor of Overland Park Christian Church (Kansas), argues that Freemasonry and Christianity are compatible.

Johns, John E., and Basil Manly IV. "Is Freemasonry Compatible with Christianity?" *Scottish Rite Journal* (February 1993): 51–54.

The authors attempt to respond to the recent controversy of the Southern Baptist Convention.

Kleinknecht, C. Fred. "Breaking the Silence." *Scottish Rite Journal* (February 1993): 3–5.

A brief response to Masonic critics.

"Masonry and Religion." *The Short Talks Bulletin* 12, no. 10 (October 1934).

McPeake, Fred W. "Southern Baptist Convention." *Scottish Rite Journal* (February 1993): 6–8.

A message urging Masons within the Southern Baptist denomination to attend the Southern Baptist Convention in June, 1993 in order to win approval of the issue of Freemasonry in the SBC.

Peale, Norman Vincent. "What Freemasonry Means to Me." *Scottish Rite Journal* (February 1993): 39–41.

Peale, author of *The Power of Positive Thinking* discusses why he is a 33rd degree Mason.

Reynolds, Herbert H. "Straight Talk." *Scottish Rite Journal* (February 1993): 64–65.

Robinson, John J. "The Southern Baptist Controversy." *The Northern Light* 24, no. 1 (February 1993): 12–16.

_____. "Who Is Dr. Holly?" *The Northern Light* 24, no. 1, (February 1993): 13–16.

Sanders, Carl J. "A Mason Without Apology." *Scottish Rite Journal* (February 1993): 59–61.

A Masonic cleric tells why he is a Mason.

Stillson, Henry L. "The Documentary Early History of the Fraternity." *History of the Ancient and Honorable Fraternity of Free and Accepted Masons*. Boston: The Fraternity Publishing Co., 1892. 167–78.

Tresner, Jim. "Conscience and the Craft." *Scottish Rite Journal* (February 1993): 13–25.

An up-to-date account of how Masons answer the questions non-Masons typically ask about the Lodge.

Wilkinson, James B. "Extremism vs. Freedom: A Masonic Call to Action." *Scottish Rite Journal* (February 1993): 9–12.

An answer to the so-called extremist critics of the Lodge.

II. Secondary Sources

A. Books

Acker, Julius W. *Strange Altars: A Scriptural Appraisal of the Lodge.* St. Louis: Concordia Publishing House, 1959.

Dated account by a Mason who left the Lodge and became a Lutheran pastor. Acker's thesis is that Freemasonry is both non-Christian and anti-Christian.

Ahlstrom, Sydney E. *A Religious History of the American People.* 2 vols. Garden City, N.Y.: Image Books, 1975.

The great Yale scholar of American religious history makes brief but insightful remarks concerning the Lodge's beginnings in America.

Ankerberg, John, and John Weldon. *The Facts on the Masonic Lodge.* Eugene, Ore.: Harvest House, 1988.

Baigent, Michael, and Richard Leigh. *The Temple and the Lodge.* New York: Arcade Publishers, 1991.

Blumenthal, Albert. *Small Town Stuff.* Chicago: University of Chicago Press, 1932.

Blumenthal discusses Freemasonry in a mining community in Colorado.

Box, H. S. *The Nature of Freemasonry.* London: Augustine Press, 1952.

An English scholar looks at Freemasonry in mid-twentieth-century England.

Brown, Harvey Newton. *Freemasonry Among Negroes and Whites in America.* El Paso, Tex.: Mereles Printing Co., 1965.

An examination of racism and the Lodge.

Byers, Dale. *I Left the Lodge.* Schaumburg, Ill.: Regular Baptist, 1989.

Cohn, Norman. *Warrant for Genocide.* New York: Harper and Row, 1967.

In addition to examining the myth of Jewish conspiracy, Cohn also seeks to dispel the myth of a Jewish-Masonic conspiracy.

Cross, Whitney. *The Burned Over District.* New York: Harper and Row, 1965.

Cross explores the beginnings of the so-called anti-Masonic era.

Daraul, Akron. *History of Secret Societies.* New York: Pocket Books, 1969.

Fisher, Paul A. *Behind the Lodge Door: Church, State, and Freemasonry.* Washington, D.C.: Shields Press, 1987.

Garitson, Elmer N. *Freemasonry: Weighed in the Balances and Found Wanting.* Middletown, Ohio: Lighthouse Publishing Co., 1990.

Hannah, Walton. *Darkness Visible.* London: Augustine Press, 1955.

An English clergyman studies the Blue Lodge and compares it to traditional Christianity, discovering the incompatibility between the church and the Lodge.

Harris, Jack. *Freemasonry: The Invisible Cult in Our Midst.* Chattanooga: Global, 1983.

Holly, James L., M.D. *The Southern Baptist Convention and Freemasonry.* Beaumont, Tex.: Mission and Ministry to Men, Inc., 1993.

In this work, the reader meets the man behind the controversy on the 1993 Southern Baptist convention.

Koch, Kurt E. *Between Christ and Satan.* Grand Rapids: Kregel Publications, 1962.

In this work, Koch contends that the Lodge has satanic origins.

_____. *Satan's Devices.* Grand Rapids: Kregel Publications, 1978.

Lochhass, Philip H. *Freemasonry in the Light of the Bible.* 1954; reprint, St. Louis: Concordia Publishing House, 1976.

McClain, Alva J. *Freemasonry and Christianity.* Winona Lake, Ind.: BMH Books, 1977.

Pickel, Theodore F., and James G. Manz. *A Christian View of Freemasonry: A Resource for Christian Thinking on Issues of Our Time.* St. Louis: Concordia Publishing House, 1957.

Roberts, J. M. *The Mythology of the Secret Societies.* New York: Charles Scribner Sons, 1972.

Rongstad, James L. *How to Respond to the Lodge.* St. Louis: Concordia Publishing House, 1977.

Schmidt, Alvin J. *The Greenwood Encyclopedia of American Institutions: Fraternal Organizations.* Westport, Conn.: Greenwood Press, 1980.

One of the most scholarly treatments on the subject of Freemasonry. Schmidt provides pertinent history and demographic information, as well as an outstanding annotated bibliography. Highly recommended.

Storms, E. M. *Should a Christian Be a Mason?* Fletcher, N.C.: New Puritan Publications, 1980.

Including a foreword by a former 33rd degree Mason, James D. Shaw, this work demonstrates the incompatibility of Christianity and Freemasonry.

B. Periodicals

Bretscher, Paul Martin. "Freemasonry and the Convocation of Canterbury." *Concordia Theological Monthly* 12, no. 8 (August 1951): 372–79.

_____. "The Masonic Apostasy from Christ." *Concordia Theological Monthly* 26, no. 2 (February 1955): 96–115.

Cohen, Abner. "The Politics of Ritual Secrecy." *Man* 6 (1971): 427–47.

Constable, John W. "Lodge Practice Within the Missouri Synod." *Concordia Theological Monthly* 39 (July–August 1968): 476–96.

A report summarizing the views of those in the Lutheran Church Missouri Synod who offer reasons why the church should remain opposed to the Lodge.

Dinegar, R. H. "Racial Crisis in De Molay." *Christian Century* 81 (March 18, 1964): 378.

> A remark concerning the apparent racism in the Order of De Molay.

Jones, Alexander E. "Mark Twain and Freemasonry." *American Literature* 2 (1954–55): 363–73.

> An extremely interesting work which shows how the Lodge exerted an influence upon one of America's most well–loved authors.

Lyttle, Charles H. "Historical Bases of Rome's Conflict with Freemasonry." *Church History* 9, no. 1 (March 1940): 3–23.

"Masonry Is Anti-Christian." *Christian News* 31, no. 21 (May 24, 1993): 1, 14–17.

> This issue of *CN* is dedicated entirely to Freemasonry and the reasons why Christians should not be Lodge members.

O'Brian, John A. "Our Friends, the Masons." *U.S. Catholic* 22 (March 1968): 25–27.

Roberts, J. M. "Freemasonry: Possibilities of a Neglected Topic." *English Historical Review* 84 (April 1969): 323–35.

Roucek, J. S. "Sociology of Secret Societies." *American Journal of Economics and Sociology* 29 (January 1960): 161–68.

Schmidt, Alvin J., and Nicholas Babchuk. "Formal Voluntary Organizations and Change Over Time: A Study of American Fraternal Organizations." *Journal of Voluntary Actions Research* (January 1972): 46–55.

_____. "The Unbrotherly Brotherhood: Discrimination in Fraternal Orders." *Phylon* 34 (Fall 1973): 275–82.

> Schmidt and Babchuk discuss the problems that the Lodge has encountered because of the racism it has practiced.

Washum, Duane. "Masonry, My Savior and Me." *Christian Research Newsletter* 1, no. 4 (1988): 1–2.

III.   Selected Masonic Periodicals

Empire State Mason
71 W. 23rd St.
New York, NY 10010

Oregon Freemason
508 Woodlark Building
Portland, OR 97205

Pennsylvania Grand Lodge Magazine
Broad and Filbert Streets
Philadelphia, PA 19107

Virginia Masonic Herald
P.O. Box 12064
Richmond, VA 23241

Texas Grand Lodge Magazine
P.O. Box 446
Waco, TX 76702

Iowa Grand Lodge Bulletin
P.O. Box 279
Cedar Rapids, IA 52406

Scottish Rite Journal
1733 Sixteenth St. N.W.
Washington, DC 20009

Indiana Freemason
P.O. Box 58
Franklin, IN 46131

Wisconsin Masonic Journal
1123 Astor St.
Milwaukee, WI 56202

Short Talks Bulletins
MSA, 8120 Fenton St.
Silver Spring, MD 20910

California Grand Lodge Magazine
1111 California St.
San Francisco, CA 94108

Philalethes Magazine
P.O. Box 402
St. Louis, MO 63108

Square and Compass
Montclair
P.O. Box 20395
Denver, CO 80220

The Northern Light
P.O. Box 519
Lexington, MA 02173

R.L.O.V. Newsletter
P.O. Box 12
Suva, Fiji

The Craftsman
Apartado 6–22
Guadalajara, 6 Jalisco
Mexico

Masonic Messenger
P.O. Box 9912
Atlanta, GA 30319

Missouri Grand Lodge Magazine
3618 Lindell Blvd
St. Louis, MO 63108

Knights Templar Magazine
14 E. Jackson Blvd.
Chicago, IL 60604

Royal Arch Mason
P.O. 529
Trenton, MO 64683

IV.   Selected List of Research Lodges

Northern California Research Lodge
1947 Tiffin Road
Oakland, CA 94602

Quatuor Coronati Lodge
27 Great Queen St.
London, W.C.2, England

Southern California Lodge of Research
10972 Sampson Ave.
Los Angeles, CA 90262

Pheonix Lodge No. 30
65 Boulevard Bineau 65
92 Neuilly-sur-Seine
Paris, France

Philosophical Lodge of Research
35 Manwaring Rd.
Niantic, CT 06357

Atlantic Lodge of Research
1690 Peachtree Street
Atlanta, GA 30309

Research Lodge No. 2
2602 Terrace Road
Des Moines, IA 50312

Missouri Lodge of Research
P.O. Box 480
Fulton, MO 65251

American Lodge of Research
71 W. 23rd St.
New York, NY 10010

Masters and Past Masters
Lodge No. 130
50 Ilam Road Riccarton
Christchurch, New Zealand

United Masters' Lodge
C.P.O. Box 564
Auckland, New Zealand

Research Lodge of Oregon
615 S.E. 62nd Ave.
Portland, OR 97215

Texas Lodge of Research
P.O. 446
Waco, TX 76703

Part V: Parallel Comparison Chart

Freemasonry	The Bible

The Bible

"The Bible is an indispensable part of the furniture of a Christian Lodge, only because it is the sacred book of the Christian religion. The Hebrew Pentateuch in a Hebrew Lodge, and the Koran in a Mohammedan one, belong on the altar" (Pike, *Morals and Dogma*, 11).

"The Bible is used among Masons as a symbol of the will of God, however it may be expressed. And, therefore, whatever to any people expresses that will may be used as a substitute for the Bible in a Masonic Lodge. Thus, in a Lodge consisting entirely of Jews, the Old Testament alone may be placed on the altar, and the Turkish Masons make use of the Koran. Whether it be the Gospels to the Christians, the Pentateuch to the Israelites, the Koran to the Muslim, or the Vedas to the Brahman, it everywhere Masonically conveys the same idea—that the symbolism of the Divine will revealed to Man" (Mackey, *Encyclopedia of Freemasonry*, 104).

"Do not add to what I command you and do not subtract from it, but keep the commands of the LORD your God that I give you" (Deut. 4:2).

"In the past God spoke to our forefathers through the prophets at many times and in various ways, but in these last days he has spoken to us by his Son, whom he appointed heir of all things, and through whom he made the universe" (Heb. 1:1–2).

"I am astonished that you are so quickly deserting the one who called you by the grace of Christ and are turning to a different gospel— which is really no gospel at all. Evidently some people are throwing you into confusion and are trying to pervert the gospel of Christ. But even if we or an angel from heaven should preach a gospel other than the one we preached to you, let him be eternally condemned. As we have already said, so now I say again: If anybody is preaching to you a gospel other than what you accepted, let him be eternally condemned!" (Gal. 1:6–9).

The Bible (cont.)

"The Bible, with all the allegories it contains, expresses, in an incomplete and veiled manner only, the religious science of the Hebrews" (Pike, *Morals and Dogma,* 744).

"There is no book of which so little is known as the Bible. To most who read it, it is as incomprehensible as the Sohar" (Pike, *Morals and Dogma,* 105).

"Your word is a lamp to my feet and a light for my path" (Ps. 119:105).

"But as for you, continue in what you have learned and have become convinced of, because you know those from whom you learned it, and how from infancy you have known the holy Scriptures, which are able to make you wise for salvation through faith in Christ Jesus" (2 Tim. 3:14–15).

"I am not ashamed of the gospel, because it is the power of God for the salvation of everyone who believes: first for the Jew, then for the Gentile" (Rom. 1:16).

"And even if our gospel is veiled, it is veiled to those who are perishing. The god of this age has blinded the minds of unbelievers, so that they cannot see the light of the gospel of the glory of Christ, who is the image of God" (2 Cor. 4:3–4).

The Doctrine of God

"Therefore it [Freemasonry] invites to its altar men of all faiths, knowing that, if they use different names for 'the Nameless One of a hundred names,' they are praying to the one God and Father of all" (*Quarterly Bulletin* [July 1915]: 17).

"This is what the LORD says—Israel's King and Redeemer, the LORD Almighty: I am the first and I am the last; apart from me there is no God" (Isa. 44:6).

"Hear, O Israel: The LORD our God, the LORD is one" (Deut. 6:4).

"Masons do not attempt to propagate any creed save their own simple and sublime one of faith in the existence of a Supreme Being and faith in His exalted works; no religion, save the universal, eternal, and immutable religion, such as God planted in the hearts of universal humanity. Masonry's followers are found alike among Christians, Jews, Brahmans, and Turks, for it is in the universal decree that: 'The one Great God looked down and smiled and counted each his loving child. For Turk and Brahman, Monk and Jew, had reached Him thru the God he knew'" (*New Age* [January 1943]: 33).

"I am the LORD your God, who brought you out of Egypt, out of the land of slavery. You shall have no other gods before me" (Ex. 20:2–3).

"Blue Lodge Masonry requires a belief in God, but no further religious belief, so that all believers in deity, whether Christians, Jews, or Mohammedans, are equally eligible for membership. It in no wise seeks to interfere with the religious beliefs of its members, and this it can only do by avoiding in its exercises the affirmation of any particular religious belief" (*Grand Lodge Proceedings of New Jersey* 23:2 [1908], 95).

"Worship the Lord your God, and serve him only" (Matt. 4:10).

"You believe that there is one God. Good! Even the demons believe that—and shudder" (James 2:19).

"All authority in heaven and on earth has been given to me [Jesus]. Therefore go and make disciples of all nations, baptizing them in the name of the Father and of the Son and of the Holy Spirit, and teaching them to obey everything I have commanded you" (Matt. 28:18–20).

The Doctrine of Jesus Christ

"Truth planted in the hearts of Socrates and Jesus grew and yielded the fruit of noble lives" (*New Age* [February 1943]: 100).

"No one Mason has the right to measure for another, within the walls of a Masonic Temple, the degree of veneration which he shall feel for any Reformer, or the Founder of any Religion" (Pike, *Morals and Dogma*, 22).

"It [Masonry] reverences all the great reformers. It sees in Moses, the Lawgiver of the Jews, in Confucius and Zoroaster, in Jesus of Nazareth, and in the Arabian Iconoclast, Great Teachers of Morality, and Eminent Reformers, if no more: and allows every brother of the Order to assign to each such higher and even Divine Character as his Creed and Truth require" (Pike, *Morals and Dogma*, 525).

"Whatever higher attributes the Founder of the Christian Faith may, in our belief, have had or not have had, none can deny that He taught and practiced a pure and elevated morality even at the risk and to the ultimate loss of his life" (Pike, *Morals and Dogma*, 308).

"It is not within the Providence of Masonry to determine how the ultimate triumph of Light and Truth and Good, over Darkness and Error and Evil, is to be achieved: nor whether the Redeemer, looked and longed for by all nations, hath appeared in Judea, or is yet to come" (Pike, *Morals and Dogma*, 525).

"Although he was a son, he learned obedience from what he suffered, and, once made perfect, he became the source of eternal salvation for all who obey him" (Heb. 5:8–9).

"Such a high priest meets our need—one who is holy, blameless, pure, set apart from sinners, exalted above the heavens" (Heb. 7:26).

"Therefore God exalted him [Jesus Christ] to the highest place and gave him the name that is above every name, that at the name of Jesus every knee should bow, in heaven and on earth and under the earth, and every tongue confess that Jesus Christ is Lord, to the glory of God the Father" (Phil. 2:9–11).

"God made him who had no sin to be sin for us, so that in him we might become the righteousness of God" (2 Cor. 5:21).

"He [Jesus] fell to the ground and prayed that if possible the hour might pass from him. 'Abba, Father,' he said, 'everything is possible for you. Take this cup from me. Yet not what I will, but what you will'" (Mark 14:35–36).

The Doctrine of Jesus Christ (cont.)

"In the Royal Arch Degree 2 Thess. 3:6–16 is read. In verses 6 and 12 the reference to Christ is omitted, and on the following page Mackey refers to this as a 'slight, but necessary modification'" (Lochhass, *Freemasonry in the Light of the Bible*, 14).

"Questions asked by Secretary, St. John's Lodge, No. 53:
1. Is it un-Masonic for a brother, while praying either in the lodge or at a burial, to close the prayer with the phrase, 'for the sake of Jesus Christ'? Answer: No. However much it may be regretted, such a question arises in the thirtieth decision of the Grand Master as to the proper conclusion of prayers at burials and in lodges, and while the Grand Master may be right in deciding that it is not un-Masonic, in the sense that charges could not be sustained for such action, in concluding Masonic prayers according to the formula of any religion, still we think that it is contrary to the spirit of Freemasonry and is in derogation of its universality, which would demand that no phrase of terms should be used in a Masonic service that would arouse sectarian feelings or wound the religious sensibilities of any Freemason" (*Grand Lodge of Texas*, December 22, 1920).

"He [Christ] has appeared once for all at the end of the ages to do away with sin by the sacrifice of himself" (Heb. 9:26).

". . . that all may honor the Son just as they honor the Father. He who does not honor the Son does not honor the Father, who sent him" (John 5:23).

"Salvation is found in no one else, for there is no other name under heaven given to men by which we must be saved. . . . But to stop this thing from spreading any further among the people, we must warn these men to speak no longer to anyone in this [Jesus'] name. Then they called them in again and commanded them not to speak or teach at all in the name of Jesus. But Peter and John replied, 'Judge for yourselves whether it is right to obey you rather than God. For we cannot help speaking about what we have seen and heard'" (Acts 4:12; 17–20).

"I tell you the truth, the man who does not enter the sheep pen by the gate, but climbs in by some other way, is a thief and a robber. . . . I am the gate for the sheep. All whoever came before me were thieves and robbers, but the sheep did not listen to them. I am the gate; whoever enters through me will be saved" (John 10:1, 7–9).

The Doctrine of Human Nature and Sin

"Nor does Masonry teach that human nature is a depraved thing, like the ruin of a once proud building. Many think that man was once a perfect being but that through some unimaginable moral catastrophe he became corrupt into the last moral fibre of his being, so that, without some kind of supernatural or miraculous help from outside him he can never of himself do, or say, or think, or be aught but that which is deformed, vile and hideous. Those who hold to this kind of anthropology usually claim to know how supernatural help may be brought to bear on the corruption which is human nature, and they usually believe that only those who accept supernatural intervention according to their own formula have any hope whatever of escaping from the original sin into which every man is born." (Haywood, *The Great Teachings of Masonry,* 138–39).

"The perfection is already within. All that is required is to remove the roughnesses and the excrescences, 'divesting our hearts and consciences of all devices and superfluities of life' to show forth the perfect man and Mason within. Thus the gavel becomes also the symbol of personal power" (Claudy, *Little Masonic Library* 4:51).

"Sin entered the world through one man, and death through sin, and in this way death came to all men, because all sinned" (Rom. 5:12).

"All have sinned and fall short of the glory of God" (Rom. 3:23).

"Surely I was a sinful at birth, sinful from the time my mother conceived me" (Ps. 51:5).

"I [Jesus] tell you the truth, no one can see the kingdom of God unless he is born again" (John 3:3).

"If we claim to be without sin, we deceive ourselves and the truth is not in us. If we confess our sins, he is faithful and just and will forgive us our sins and purify us from all unrighteousness. If we claim we have not sinned, we make him out to be a liar and his word has no place in our lives" (1 John 1:8–10).

The Doctrine of Human Nature and Sin (cont.)

"Man also contains within him a life-force, a 'vital and immortal Principle' as Masonry calls it, which has not yet expanded to full development in him, and indeed in many men is scarcely active at all. Man, too, has that in him enabling him to evolve from the stage of the mortal animal to a being immortal, superhuman, godlike. ... Human evolution can be accelerated if not at present in the mass of humanity, yet in suitable individuals. Human nature is perfectible by an intensive process of purification and initiation" (Wilmhurst, *The Masonic Initiation*, 27–28).

"All of us have become like one who is unclean, and all our righteous acts are like filthy rags; we all shrivel up like a leaf, and like the wind our sins sweep us away" (Isa. 64:6).

"We know that the law is spiritual; but I am unspiritual, sold as a slave to sin. I do not understand what I do. For what I want to do I do not do, but what I hate I do" (Rom. 7:14–15).

"We all, like sheep, have gone astray, each of us has turned to his own way" (Isa. 53:6).

The Doctrine of Salvation

"If true religion is thus to be narrowed down to salvation in no other name under heaven, and St. Paul's words to this effect be understood in a spirit of bigoted literalness, then any such 'Christian' must indeed be straining his conscience to the breaking point by accepting initiation into the broader and deeper mysteries of Freemasonry. *I, for one, can never understand how anyone who takes an exclusive view of Christ as the only complete revelation of God's truth can become a Freemason without suffering from spiritual schizophrenia*" (Vindex, *Light Invisible*, 24–27 [emphasis added]).

"Salvation is found in no one else; for there is no other name under heaven given to men by which we must be saved" (Acts 4:12).

"No one can serve two masters. Either he will hate the one and love the other, or he will be devoted to the one and despise the other" (Matt. 6:24).

"If serving the LORD seems undesirable to you, then choose for yourselves this day whom you will serve. ... But as for me and my household, we will serve the LORD" (Josh. 24:15).

"He who doubts is like a wave of the sea, blown and tossed by the wind. That man should not think he will receive anything from the Lord; he is a double-minded man, unstable in all he does" (James 1:6–8).

The Doctrine of Salvation (cont.)

"If any member of our fraternity acknowledges his faith in a Supreme Being, whose law is his guide, and strives honestly to live by his faith, we care not what the other articles of his creed may be, for we believe that when summoned from this sublunary abode, he will be received into the all-perfect, celestial lodge above, for he will, by his life, have made of earth the porch-way into heaven" (Thorpe, *Royal Arch,* n.p.).

"There he [the initiate] stands without our portals, on the threshold of this new Masonic life, in darkness, helplessness, and ignorance. Having been wandering amid the errors and covered only with the pollutions of the outer and profane world, he comes inquiringly into our doors, seeking the new birth, and for asking withdrawal of the veil which conceals divine Truth from his uninitiated sight" (*Masonic Ritualist,* n.p.).

Masonry "inculcates the practice of virtue but it applies no scheme of redemption for sin. It points its disciples to the path of righteousness" (Mackey, *Encyclopedia of Freemasonry,* 619).

"For God so loved the world that he gave his one and only Son, *that whoever believes in him shall not perish* but have eternal life" (John 3:16 [emphasis added]).

"For they mouth empty, boastful words and, by appealing to the lustful desires of sinful human nature, they entice people who are just escaping from those who live in error. . . . If they have escaped the corruption of the world by knowing our Lord and Savior Jesus Christ and are again entangled in it and overcome, they are worse off at the end than they were at the beginning" (2 Peter 2:18, 20).

"Whoever believes in him is not condemned, but whoever does not believe stands condemned already because he has not believed in the name of God's one and only Son" (John 3:18).

[Jesus says] "Here I am! I stand at the door and knock. If anyone hears my voice and opens the door, I will come in and eat with him, and he with me" (Rev. 3:20).

"I [Jesus] tell you the truth, no one can see the kingdom of God unless a man is born again. . . . I tell you the truth, no one can enter the kingdom of God unless he is born of water and the Spirit " (John 3:3, 5).

"What shall we conclude then? Are we any better? Not at all! We have already made the charge that Jews and Gentiles alike are all under sin. As it is written: 'There is no one righteous, not even one'" (Rom. 3:9–10).

The Doctrine of Salvation (cont.)

"We find in the Masonic funeral service an allusion to a certain 'pass' whereby we may obtain entrance into the Grand Lodge above. What higher conception could we have of the Master's Word than the pass whereby we can find immortality and entrance into the Grand Lodge on high? We are told that this pass is the pass of a pure and blameless life" (Ball, *The Builder,* 1:287).

"The Sword, pointing to a naked heart, demonstrates that justice will sooner or later overtake us; and although our thoughts, words, and actions may be hidden from the eyes of man, yet that All-Seeing Eye Whom the Sun, Moon and Stars obey, and under whose watchful care even Comets perform their stupendous revolutions, pervades the inmost recesses of the human heart and will reward us according to our merits" (*King Solomon and His Followers,* Missouri, 157).

"The one great God operating the universe has a place for every one of his sons whom he created. To think that Christians only merit immortality is narrow and not in keeping with the omnipotent love of the Creator of this vast universe" (Van Cott, *Masonic Inspiration* 1, no. 9 [July 1955]).

"I am not ashamed of the gospel, because it is the power of God for the salvation of everyone who believes: first for the Jew, then for the Gentile. For in the gospel a righteousness from God is revealed, a righteousness that is by faith from first to last, just as it is written: 'The righteous will live by faith' " (Rom. 1:16–17).

"I [Jesus] tell you the truth, the man who does not enter the sheep pen by the gate, but climbs in by some other way, is a thief and a robber. The man who enters by the gate is the shepherd of his sheep. The watchman opens the gate for him, and the sheep listen to his voice. . . . I am the gate; whoever enters through me will be saved" (John 10:1–3, 9).

"For it is by grace you have been saved, through faith—and this not from yourselves, it is the gift of God—not by works, so that no one can boast" (Eph. 2:8–9).

"What then shall we say that Abraham, our forefather, discovered in this matter? If, in fact, Abraham was justified by works, he had something to boast about—but not before God. What does the Scripture say? 'Abraham believed God, and it was credited to him as righteousness' " (Rom. 4:1–3).

"Do not let your hearts be troubled. Trust in God; trust also in me. . . . I am the way and the truth and the life. No one comes to the Father except through me" (John 14:1, 6).

79

The Doctrine of Salvation (cont.)

"Is Masonry anti-Christian? No, Masonry is not anti any religion. . . . Masonry encourages its members in their individual faiths. Masons do not oppose any faith." (Tresner, "Conscience and the Craft," *Scottish Rite Journal* [February 1993]): 17.

"Because Masonry does not deal with salvation, what is the relevance of its members' various views on the subject? It is the beauty of Masonry that good people, regardless of religious beliefs may gather and share those timeless truths about human nature that are common to all great religions. For me, one of the enjoyments I derive from Masonry is the opportunity to share with Jews, Muslims, and others those timeless truths regarding ethical conduct and to deepen my own personal faith and understanding of God with the help of the added perspectives of others who believe with possibly different interpretations. Masonry . . . unites; it does not divide. It respects all people and does not seek to replace the religions of any of them, nor claim that some are superior to others" (Doan, "An Open Letter," *Scottish Rite Journal* [February 1993]: 43).

"Elijah went before the people and said, 'How long will you waver between two opinions? If the Lord is God, follow him; but if Baal is God, follow him' " (1 Kings 18:21).

"We should not think that the divine being is like gold or silver or stone—an image made by man's design and skill. In the past God overlooked such ignorance, but now he commands all people everywhere to repent. For he has set a day when he will judge the world with justice by the man he has appointed. He has given proof of this to all men by raising him from the dead" (Acts 17:29–31).

"Do not suppose that I have come to bring peace to the earth. I did not come to bring peace, but a sword. For I have come to turn 'a man against his father, a daughter against her mother, a daughter-in-law against her mother-in-law—a man's enemies will be the members of his own household'" (Matt. 10:34–36).

The Occult

"Much light, it must be confessed, is thrown on many of the mystical names in the higher degrees by these dogmas of magic; and hence magic furnishes a curious and interesting study for the Freemason" (Mackey, *Encyclopedia of Freemasonry*, 459).

"Freemasonry and alchemy have sought the same results, the lesson of Divine Truth and the doctrine of immortal life, and they have both sought it by the same methods of symbolism. It is not, therefore, strange that in the eighteenth century, and perhaps before, we find an incorporation of much of the science of alchemy into that of Freemasonry" (Mackey, *Encyclopedia of Freemasonry,* 44).

"The Kaballa may be defined to be a system of philosophy which embraces certain mystical interpretations of Scripture, and metaphysical speculations concerning the Deity, man, and spiritual things. Much use is made of it in the high degrees, and entire rites have been constructed on its principles. Hence it demands a place in my general work on Masonry" (Mackey, *Encyclopedia of Freemasonry,* 375).

"Let no one be found among you who . . . practices divination or sorcery, interprets omens, engages in witchcraft, or casts spells, or who is a medium or spiritist or who consults the dead" (Deut. 18:10–11; cf. Ex. 7; 8; Lev. 19:31; 1 Sam. 28).

"See to it that no one takes you captive through hollow and deceptive philosophy, which depends on human tradition and the basic principles of this world rather than on Christ" (Col. 2:8).

"Command certain men not to teach false doctrines any longer nor to devote themselves to myths and endless geneologies. These promote controversies rather than God's work—which is by faith" (1 Tim. 1:3–4).

"To suit their own desires, they will gather around them a great number of teachers to say what their itching ears want to hear. They will turn their ears away from the truth and turn aside to myths" (2 Tim. 4:3–4).

"We did not follow cleverly invented stories when we told you about the power and coming of our Lord Jesus Christ . . ." (2 Peter 1:16).

81

Oaths

"Mr. ____, upon entering the Lodge for the first time, receive you on the point of a sharp instrument pressing your naked left breast, which is to teach you, as this is an instrument of torture to your flesh, so should the recollection of it ever be to your mind and conscience should you attempt to reveal the secrets of Masonry unlawfully" (Whalen, *Handbook of Secret Organizations*, 57).

"... binding myself under no less penalty than that of having my throat cut from ear to ear, my tongue torn out by its roots and buried in the rough sands of the sea at low water mark where the tide ebbs and flows twice in twenty-four hours, should I ever knowingly or willingly violate this my solemn oath and obligation as an Entered Apprentice Mason. So help me God, and keep me steadfast in the due performance of the same" (*King Solomon and His Followers*, 22).

"You cannot cast away your stone. It is yourself. You cannot evade it and its responsibilities by resigning and remaining absent from the Brotherhood in which you first acquired the stone. Once a Mason, always a Mason: in this world and in worlds to come. You stand solemnly and eternally covenanted, not only to yourself and your Brotherhood, but to the Eternal Sacred Law, to proceed with your Masonic work to the end. That Law does not permit you to stultify an obligation deliberately made upon It, even if made ignorantly" (*King Solomon and His Followers*, 153).

"Come to me [Jesus], all you who are weary and burdened, and I will give you rest. Take my yoke upon you and learn from me, for I am gentle and humble in heart, and you will find rest for your souls. For my yoke is easy and my burden is light" (Matt 11:28–30).

"You shall not misuse the name of the LORD your God, for the LORD will not hold anyone guiltless who misuses his name" (Ex. 20:7).

"Above all, my brothers, do not swear—not by heaven or by earth or by anything else. Let your 'Yes' be yes, and your 'No,' no, or you will be condemned" (James 5:12).

"You have heard that it was said to the people long ago, 'Do not break your oath, but keep the oaths you have made to the Lord.' But I [Jesus] tell you, Do not swear at all: either by heaven, for it is God's throne; or by the earth, for it is his footstool; or by Jerusalem, for it is the city of the Great King. And do not swear by your head, for you cannot make even one hair white or black. Simply let your 'Yes' be 'Yes,' and your 'No,' 'No'; anything beyond this comes from the evil one" (Matt. 5:33–37).

Racism

"There are excellent reasons for this apparent race discrimination which only a Mason can fully understand; suffice it to say here that, feelings being what they are, that such a step would endanger the harmony of the lodge, which is a very primary consideration. Secondly, although Negroes today may technically fulfill the Masonic Requirement, being "free," their subordinate economic, educational, and cultural position is such that they hardly fulfill the spirit of that prerequisite to initiation" (Vindex, *Light Invisible*, 1952).*

"For God so loved the *world* that he gave his one and only Son, that *whoever* believes in him shall not perish but have eternal life" (John 3:16 [emphasis added]).

"You are all sons of God through faith in Christ Jesus, for all of you who were baptized into Christ have clothed yourselves with Christ. There is neither Jew nor Greek, slave nor free, male nor female, for you are all one in Christ Jesus" (Gal. 3:26–28).

---

* It should be noted that some modern Masons do indeed repudiate racism, but published statements to this effect are uncommon.